Macroeconomic Policies and the Development of Markets in Transition Economies

Macroeconomic Policies and the Development of Markets in Transition Economies

Fabrizio Coricelli

Central European University Press

Budapest

© 1998 by the Privatization Project

ISBN 963 9116 05 X Cloth

Central European University Press
Október 6. utca 12.
H-1051 Budapest
Hungary

Printed in Hungary

To my parents

Contents

Acknowledgments ix

Introduction 1

1 Stabilization, Liberalization, and Macroeconomic
Performance 8

2 Monetary Policy and Financial Markets in
Transition Economies 37

3 Macroeconomic Constraints and Feedback 86

4 Income Distribution and the Dynamics of Reform 135

Notes 147

References 153

Index 161

Acknowledgments

I am particularly indebted to Guillermo Calvo, Bankim Chadha, and Simon Commander, coauthors of many ideas reflected in this book. They all made my work on transition economies an extraordinarily rewarding job. Special thanks go to Roman Frydman, who encouraged me to write this book. He has had a great influence on my work through a continuous exchange of ideas that started in 1990. In addition, his passionate interest about economies in transition and his creative thinking on these economies always was a great stimulus for me to study the economics of transition. The book reflects research carried out within the Central European University Macroeconomics Program of the Privatization Project.

Introduction

Paul Krugman recently reminded us about a memorable comment made by Paul Samuelson, who "cautioned against basing economic policy on 'shibboleths,' by which he meant slogans that take the place of hard thinking. . . . The Oxford English Dictionary defines a shibboleth as a 'catchword or formula adopted by a party or sect, by which their adherents or followers may be excluded.' Simplistic ideas in economics often become badges of identity for groups of like-minded people, who repeat certain phrases to each other, and eventually mistake repetition for truth" (*Economist*, 31 August 1996).

The experience of reforms in previously centrally planned economies (PCPEs) is not immune to these slogans. Different views tend to be classified under simple headings, such as gradualist, populist, shock therapist, or follower of soft policies. This is inevitable when economic ideas are used by policymakers and when vested interests hide themselves behind "objective economic reasons." Furthermore, the role of economic advice, often coming from Western advisers, has been extremely important in PCPEs. Not only reform programs were launched under the umbrella of IMF and World Bank agreements. The absolute lack of experience in market reform forced countries to ask for advice on every matter concerning economic and institutional reforms (see Blejer and Coricelli 1995).

Notwithstanding these justifications, it remains true that the historical transformation taking place in Central and Eastern Europe deserves a more careful, perhaps more detached analysis. Dewatripont and Roland (1996) have recently noted that "the ratio of theory to policy papers in transition economics has . . . been surprisingly low." We would stress here that this phenomenon was somehow inevitable, because of the objective difficulty in building a theory of transition. The object of the analysis—transition—is not well defined. The toolbox of instruments at the disposal of economists is not well suited to analyzing such phenomena. The workhorse of modern economics, the Walrasian general equilibrium model, is largely irrelevant to analyzing a process of "large-scale institutional change" (as defined in Dewatripont and Roland 1996). Rather than achieving equilibria in a well-functioning market system, transition is mainly a process of market creation. It is not an accident that the most influential theoretical work on transition has been in the analysis of large-scale privatization and the imposition of clear property rights (Frydman and Rapaczynski 1994). An important strand of literature on microeconomic incentives has developed, with interesting implications for such issues as enterprise and bank restructuring, the role of soft budget constraints, and others. Moreover, important insights can be found in the political economy literature. Dewatripont and Roland (1996) offer an excellent review of the microeconomic incentives and the literature on political economy. Extremely stimulating as well have been the views put forward by Murrell (1995, 1996) on an evolutionary approach to transition. It is unfortunate that most researchers of transition have avoided opening a fruitful dialogue with proponents of the evolutionary approach.

While on the microeconomic front an embryonic development of a theory of transition can be seen, on the macroeconomic front the picture is quite different. Having benefitted from numerous experiences of stabilization programs in developing and developed economies, economists had a set of recipes to sell to transition countries. It is thus widely accepted that in the areas of macroeconomic stabilization and macroeconomic policy, economies in transition differ very little from market economies.

Although there are several macroeconomic phenomena that can be studied in a similar way for very different historical and institutional contexts (high inflation, for instance), in this book we partly disagree with the above view. Indeed, the distinguishing feature of this book is our argument that the specific institutional characteristics of PCPEs have important implications for macroeconomic policy design and for the effects of macroeconomic policy during transition.

It is impossible to cite the numerous important contributions to the economics of transition. The pressure of unfolding events and the novelty of the experience, however, have been an obstacle to systematic analysis. In this book we try to sketch a unified view of transition. We attempt to develop a simple framework of

2

transition that stresses the interplay between institutional aspects linked to the previous regime and macroeconomic outcomes of the transition period.[1] Although the analytical framework for this book was coauthored in a previous work, this book brings together different areas of research, particularly stabilization analysis and the dynamic adjustment and growth process. The central idea guiding the current analysis is that economic performance results from a rather complex interaction between initial conditions (history) and changes (policy reforms).

To avoid misunderstanding of our views, we want to state up front that structural and institutional reforms are not a substitute for sound macroeconomic policies. However, the converse is true as well: tough macroeconomic policies are not a substitute for institutional reforms and market creation.

Paradoxically, the fact that we are dealing with a transition process is often neglected in much current analysis. Indeed, transition involves peculiar features in terms of the nonlinear path of the main economic aggregates and peculiar intertemporal issues. Moreover, a key aspect of transition is the development of markets and market institutions. Thus, policies and outcomes should be assessed not only by short-term macroeconomic indicators, but also in terms of their impact on the development of markets. For instance, it is conceivable that certain policies may sustain output growth in the short run but will hamper the development of markets and market institutions, thus harming long-run growth. Privatization policies are a case in point. Faster privatization may adversely affect output in the short run while still increasing the long-run growth potential of the economy.

These issues are relevant as well to macroeconomic policies, such as credit policy and fiscal policy. An important implication is that looking at the problems in isolation from the overall transition path can be misleading.

Within this perspective, transition is a process entailing several trade-offs between short-term costs and long-term benefits. This leads to problems in political economy affecting support for reforms, some of which are connected with intergenerational problems. Indeed, if transition is a costly process that yields long-run benefits, the older generations may live only long enough to see the costly period. Intergenerational equity calls for a transfer from younger generations to older generations. However, governments have generally focused on short-term budgetary problems.

3

Ex post, they in fact surrendered to the pressures of pensioners, ending up with unsustainable pension systems. Instead of directly dealing with the issue of compensation for potential losers of transition, governments reacted ex post to pressure groups by boosting expenditures on ill-designed systems of pensions and social assistance.

This book discusses macroeconomic issues within an overall framework of transition. First, it analyzes the implementation of stabilization and price liberalization policies. Reviewing empirical evidence of the experiences of twenty-six countries, chapter 1 shows that stabilization policies exacerbated the (probably inevitable) output decline. This was mainly due to the contraction of bank credit in the context of severely underdeveloped financial systems. The less developed the market institutions were, the more acute the adverse effect of stabilization policies.

The second part of chapter 1 analyzes the adjustment period after the initial stabilization phase. Macroeconomic performance, both in terms of inflation and of output, varied markedly across countries. In contrast with recent analyses that attribute better macroeconomic performance to faster liberalization and reform measures, we found that initial conditions, in terms of economic liberalization and the state of the private sector, played a key role. Indeed, in a regression of output performance after liberalization, we added an indicator of initial conditions—in terms of economic liberalization (computed by the World Bank) prior to the reforms of the 1990s—to cumulative liberalization and a dummy for countries affected by war. We found that initial conditions are important and statistically significant.

By contrast, the significance of cumulative liberalization—noted by the World Bank (1994) and Sachs (1996)—disappears when initial conditions are included. We interpret this result as an indication of how important at least a minimal market structure and market behaviors are for the performance of economies in transition. This can be interpreted as an evolutionary element (see Murrell 1996) in the process of transition, which indicates that abrupt destruction of economic relations may be very costly. Reform policies should take initial conditions into account. Indeed, private markets may arise when there is a conducive underlying structure (trade credit in Hungary and Poland, for instance). Otherwise, dysfunctional institutions can arise and continue to operate.

4

Chapter 2 focuses on the financial market. It develops a simple framework to discuss the role of credit markets in the transition from central planning, where financial markets played no role, to a market-based economy. The main hypothesis is that the underdevelopment of financial markets implies the crucial role of liquidity in determining output in these economies. Industrial structures were rigid, with interfirm linkages hard to change in the short run. In extreme cases, before reforms, the whole economy was functioning as a unique vertically integrated sector. Monetary exchanges and credit contracts were irrelevant for the operation of the system. After reforms were instituted, interfirm exchanges came to take place through monetary transfers, either payments on delivery or delayed payments (trade credit). In a developed industrial structure, most firms are both suppliers to some firms and customers of other firms. The higher the degree of "circularity" of the system, the higher the exposure of the system to local shocks. The financial difficulties of one firm can be transmitted to the entire system through linking the firms together. The only financial alternative to trade credit was bank credit. A key question to analyze is, what happened when bank credit was sharply restricted at the outset of reforms? Under "normal" circumstances, the withdrawal of the central bank as *lender of last resort* should have increased the risk in any credit market, including trade credit. All sources of credit should have contracted, creating serious financial difficulties for firms. However, the experience has been heterogeneous across countries. In some countries, the contraction of bank credit was accompanied by the blossoming of interenterprise arrears. While these arrears may have softened the initial crunch, they entailed large social costs. Arrears are different from voluntary trade credit, and, in fact, they can hamper the development of an efficient trade credit market. In other countries—for example, Poland—interenterprise credit fell together with bank credit.

The liquidity aspect of credit-monetary policy in PCPEs has been largely understated. More attention has been devoted to the disciplining role of credit markets. However, the liquidity and the discipline aspects of credit policy cannot be separated. Indeed, both loose and excessively tight credit policies can lead to negative effects on output as well as on "market discipline." Excessive tightening of credit policy may lead to generalized default and a consequent lack of discipline, followed by a loosening of policy to avoid a financial collapse. Such a situation is analogous to the progressive "demonetization" of an economy determined by runaway inflation in the context of an automatically accommodative monetary policy.

The response of the economy to sudden credit/monetary tightening depends on the initial conditions of economic structure and institutional development. Particularly important is the role played by private trade credit markets in response to the break-up of traditional automatic financing operated by the banks. Note that throughout economic history, bank credit followed the development of trade credit. Centralization of credit developed out of the seeds of the decentralized credit arrangements created by individual traders. The experience of economies in transition reversed such a sequence. Under central planning, trade credit was generally forbidden by law. With market reforms, the highly centralized credit is suddenly frozen, and firms are left to their own initiative to regulate their transactions and credit arrangements. Not surprisingly, the functioning of private credit markets crucially depends on a minimum market structure that imposes credible penalties for "bad" behavior and rewards for "good" behavior. In this respect, these countries started from highly heterogenous initial conditions, which, we argue, had a decisive impact on the effects of the similar macroeconomic policies that were applied.

Chapter 3 analyzes transition as a process of massive reallocation of resources across sectors and firms. Such a process contains elements of evolution, as new firms emerge and absorb resources from the old, declining firms and of policy design, as firms are privatized, restructured, or closed by state intervention.[2] The dynamics of the economy crucially depend on the weight of these elements. The inherited economic structure and capital stock play a fundamental role in the process. How much of such capital—including both human and physical—can be used in the new market environment?

The model we develop in this chapter illustrates the various transition paths that can emerge from different initial conditions in terms of human and physical capital stock. It appears that the less favorable the initial conditions, the higher the unemployment cost of transition. There is a crucial trade-off between unemployment and overall restructuring of the economy. However, unemployment cannot be considered an unconstrained variable.

Indeed, there are fiscal and political economy effects of unemployment that can lead to a maximum tolerable rate of unemployment. This chapter shows that the opposition to sustained fast reforms can grow together with the increase in unemployment. However, focusing only on unemployment may be misleading.

Chapter 4 identifies another channel affecting the speed of reform and pressures for policy reversal. Support for restructuring and fast reforms is likely to be affected as well by developments in the real income of the population. As stressed in the development and growth literature, a primary factor affecting political attitudes is the degree of inequality in income distribution.

The transition model developed in chapter 4 generates a Kuznets curve that parallels the bell-shaped curve showing the behavior of unemployment during transition. The value added gained from analyzing the behavior of income distribution during transition is given by the possibility of a nonsynchronized behavior of income distribution, output growth, and unemployment. Specifically, inequality may continue to increase well beyond the turning point of output and unemployment. This may help to explain the apparent paradox of dissatisfaction with reformist governments in countries in which the economy was undergoing a significant recovery of output, as was the case in Poland.

More generally, the model permits an analysis of the behavior of income distribution in a system in which relative wages, employment in the two sectors, and unemployment are endogenous and vary over time.

1

Stabilization, Liberalization, and Macroeconomic Performance

1. Introduction

By 1996, twenty-six countries of Central and Eastern Europe and the former Soviet Union (fSU) had embarked on stabilization programs and market-oriented reforms. A main feature, unexpected at least in its magnitude, was the collapse of output in all stabilization programs. There is little doubt that the decline in output in PCPEs was due mainly to systemic factors. The dismantling of the old system of economic relations and coordination was replaced by a market-based system without, however, having the necessary market institutions and coordination mechanisms in place for an efficiently functioning market economy. Does this imply that macroeconomic policies were irrelevant? Quite the contrary. It implies that macroeconomic policies were far from neutral. Indeed, in the institutional vacuum created by market reforms without markets, government policy played a key role. A corollary of this view is that even though only a small proportion of the output decline can be explained by economic policy, the adverse effects of such policies were particularly important because they added hardship to an already severely hit economy.

Despite a superficial homogeneity of experiences, country strategies and performance have been extremely different. This chapter analyzes both similarities and differences by looking at the design of stabilization programs and the different pace of liberalization and structural reform.

Macroeconomic stabilization was a key component of market reforms. Indeed, most planned economies suffered from large fiscal and external imbalances and accompanying inflationary pressures, either open or hidden by price controls. At the outset of reforms, policymakers faced three fundamental choices in the design of stabilization policies.

First, there was the choice between exchange-rate-based stabilization programs (ERBs) and money-based stabilization programs (MBs). The experience of market economies indicates that the two programs yield different outcomes in terms of the speed of the decline of inflation and in terms of the output costs. Exchange-rate-based programs tend to produce a faster decline in inflation and a lower, if any, drop in output. However, for many countries fixing the exchange rate was not a feasible option, because they lacked a sufficient stock of foreign reserves necessary to support the peg. A key question is why international institutions, primarily the International Monetary Fund, did not push countries to adopt fixed exchange rate programs and did not contribute to providing them with exchange rate stabilization funds, like the one established for Poland in 1990. The case for the exchange rate anchor was even stronger in economies in transition. Indeed, the lack of tested instruments for monetary policy rendered inefficient the use of money supply as the main instrument of policy.

Notwithstanding these considerations, this chapter shows that the choice of the nominal anchor was not crucial for the performance of the economies. Output collapsed in every country, irrespective of the type of program adopted. We argue that the potential advantages of ERBs were not exploited because of major mistakes in the accompanying policies, mainly in credit policies and the exchange rate devaluation that preceded the fixing of the exchange rate. In contrast with the same rationale for the use of the exchange rate as a nominal anchor, programs generally set excessively tight credit ceilings or interest rates. There was major confusion between stocks and flows and between a jump in the price level and rates of inflation. In the face of a huge jump in the price level, the nominal stock of credit was initially kept constant.

9

In some cases, as in Poland, interest rates were targeted to the rate of inflation that included the initial jump in the price level. The result was that interest rates were negative ex post—measured in relation to past or contemporaneous inflation—but positive and very high ex ante—measured in relation to expected inflation, after the initial price-level jump.

Although a verdict on the empirical relevance of the credit squeeze is still open, it is hardly disputable that a contraction in real credit and monetary aggregates of the magnitude observed in economies in transition should have exerted a recessionary impact. Our conclusion is that the stock of credit and money should have accommodated the initial jump in the price level. Thereafter, the rate of growth of money and credit should have been reduced to the targeted rates of inflation, after the initial price-level jump. The Yugoslav program at the end of 1989 and the beginning of 1990 was indeed designed in this way and worked very well initially, before political factors destroyed the program (Coricelli and Rocha 1991). The alternative of delaying price liberalization or carrying out a gradual liberalization of prices would have led to anticipatory behavior by economic actors and likely would have produced large imbalances and worsened shortages, as consumers and firms would have accumulated inventories of durable goods.

The second important choice is related to the implementation of income or wage policy. The same considerations used to argue in favor of the exchange rate anchor could apply to the use of wage policy as an additional nominal anchor. Income policies have been an important element of successful exchange rate stabilization programs in market economies (as in Israel and Mexico in the 1980s). In economies in transition there are additional microeconomic considerations in favor of the adoption of income policies. In particular, in state-owned enterprises the bargaining power of the owner (the state) was very weak, leading to excessive power for insiders. Moreover, given the severe underdevelopment of financial markets, firms were liquidity constrained. In that context, wage behavior was crucial in affecting the ability of firms to accumulate monetary balances and finance their activities (see Calvo and Coricelli 1992).

The third important issue in the design of macroeconomic policies is related to the mix between fiscal and monetary policy stances. Fiscal policy in economies in transition does not entail simply the control of the budget deficit, but also involves the issue of reducing the role of the state in the economy. A key aspect of the initial stages of reform is the extent and speed of the reduction of subsidies that were central to the operation of the economy under the old regime. Cutting subsidies to firms and consumers was the key step in abandoning soft budget constraints, based on a cross-subsidization of firms. The reallocation of resources induced by the cut in subsidies necessitated credit. Thus, an overly tight credit policy at the outset of reforms was in conflict with the needed adjustments in production, probably interfering with the beneficial effects that hard budget constraints (via elimination of subsidies) would have brought. Again, the fundamental importance of cutting subsidies, including those on the flow of credit, was confused with a contraction of the initial stock of credit. In sum, macroeconomic policies that should have accompanied price liberalization were generally flawed. This likely contributed to the large initial fall in output.

The second part of this chapter focuses on the post-stabilization phase. The adjustment following the initial shock has been heterogeneous across countries. Macroeconomic performance has been much better in countries of Central and Eastern Europe than in countries of the fSU. Reviewing the cross-country evidence, we conclude that initial conditions, rather than reform policies, played a crucial role. In contrast to the growing consensus on the link between liberalization, speed of reform, and positive macroeconomic outcome, we suggest that the presence of a minimal set of market institutions was the key to the relative success of market reforms (see Murrell 1996 for a similar view). Lacking such a minimum structure, the application of "big bang" policies produced a persistent output decline in several countries as well as and the development of dysfunctional institutions and behaviors. Generalized interenterprise arrears, barter, and even the explosive growth of the mafia may be seen as examples of such dysfunctional institutions (see Cohen 1995).

2. Reform strategies: Stabilization, Liberalization, and Institutional Reforms

Reform programs differed significantly across countries. First, stabilization programs differed in terms of the main instruments and intermediate targets adopted. Table 1.1 shows that out of twenty-

Table 1.1

Stabilization and Exchange Rate Regime in Transition Economies

Country	Exchange rate adopted
Albania	Flexible
Armenia	Flexible/Fixed
Azerbaijan	Flexible/Fixed
Belarus	Flexible/Fixed
Bulgaria	Flexible
Croatia	Fixed
Czech Republic	Fixed
Estonia	Fixed
Georgia	Flexible/Fixed
Hungary	Fixed
Kazakhstan	Flexible/Fixed
Kyrgyz Republic	Flexible/Fixed
Latvia	Flexible/Fixed
Lithuania	Flexible/Fixed
Macedonia, fYR	Fixed
Moldova	Flexible
Mongolia	Flexible
Poland	Fixed
Romania	Flexible
Russia	Flexible/Fixed
Slovak Republic	Fixed
Slovenia	Flexible
Tajikistan	Flexible
Turkmenistan	Not applicable
Ukraine	Flexible
Uzbekistan	Flexible

Source: IMF (1996)

six reforming countries, six adopted the exchange rate as the nominal anchor, while twenty used money supply as the main tool to control inflation, at least in their first stabilization attempt. However, irrespective of the exchange rate regime, most countries relied on wage policy as an accompanying nominal anchor. Second, the pace of liberalization of prices and of foreign trade varied significantly across countries. Finally, the speed and extent of institutional reforms in the areas of enterprise and the financial sector varied widely from country to country.

Regarding these structural and institutional aspects, several quantitative measures of different reform indicators have been recently computed (see De Melo et al. 1995 and EBRD 1995).[1] It is thus possible to classify countries according to the values of different indicators. Of course, such an attempt to quantify complex phenomena should be made with caution. Nevertheless, the indicators provide a useful framework to organize the experience of more than twenty countries.[2]

Reform strategies can be classified along two main dimensions: the design of stabilization programs and the speed and extent of structural and institutional reforms, summarized by liberalization indicators.

Given the short time span of the postreform period, it is hard to separate the role of stabilization measures from liberalization and more structural measures. The drawbacks arising from the lack of time series observations can be partly overcome by using cross-country data. However, cross-country analysis must take into account that countries began their reforms in a nonsynchronized manner. We begin with an overview of the role and operation of stabilization programs.

2.1 Macroeconomic Stabilization

Studies of stabilization programs in market economies have reached a consensus on the fact that the effects on the real economy and on the speed of adjustment of inflation vary significantly between ERBs and MBs. In addition to the design of stabilization programs, it has been noted that the performance of the economy following stabilization critically depends on the nature of inflation. In particular, Kiguel and Liviatan (1991) distinguish chronic from nonchronic inflation and emphasize that the choice of different instruments and nominal anchors should take into account the nature of the underlying inflationary process.

Broadly speaking, it has been found that MBs tend to be associated with a recession at the outset of stabilization. Moreover, the speed of decline of inflation tends to be slower in MBs. In contrast, ERBs do not cause a recession at the beginning of stabilization. In fact, sometimes a temporary boost to output—and especially consumption—is observed. Furthermore, in ERBs, the rate of inflation falls rapidly.

Thus, evidence from market economies illustrates the short-term advantages in terms of speed of decline in inflation and low output costs of ERBs. However, in extending the analysis beyond the first stage of stabilization, it was found that ERBs ran into difficulties later on. Exchange-rate-based stabilizations ran through a cycle of initial increase in output followed by a recession. Thus, different stabilization programs seem to yield different paths of output, rather than different cumulative effects on output. The time dimension is therefore crucial in evaluating the effects of different programs.

Despite some analogies, a closer look at the evidence shows that the experience of countries in transition differed sharply from that of market economies, especially in connection with output behavior. The clear-cut distinction between the dynamics of output in MBs and ERBs was not observed in economies in transition, in which stabilization invariably led to an initial sharp output decline. The adoption of a stabilization program was not a necessary condition for output decline, as output fell even in countries

Figure 1.1

Output Fall During the Year of Stabilization

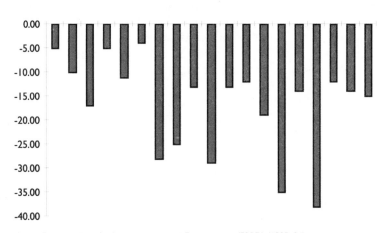

Source: European Bank for Reconstruction and Development (EBRD) (1995–96)

that did not implement stabilization, or sometimes output began to fall before the implementation of stabilization programs. However, stabilization programs seem to be a sufficient condition for output decline. Indeed, the implementation of a stabilization program coincided with decline in output, or an acceleration of it in those cases where the recession started before stabilization (figure 1.1).

2.2 Design of Stabilization Programs and Macroeconomic Performance

Although there is significant variation within each group, transition economies broadly confirm the findings for market economies.[3] When feasible, the implementation of the exchange

Figure 1.2

Exchange Rate Regime and Inflation

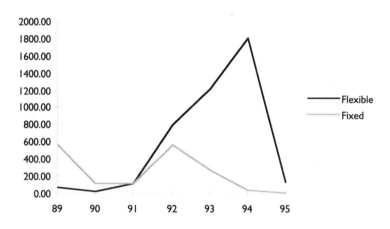

Source: EBRD (1995–96)

rate as a nominal anchor seems to facilitate—with respect to money-based programs—the reduction of inflation, both in terms of the speed of the decline and the level at which the inflation rate stabilizes (figure 1.2).

However, the dynamics of real variables seem to be rather different in transition economies. In particular, the initial favorable effect on consumption—and often output—of ERBs was not

15

Figure 1.3

Output Changes and Exchange Rate Regime, 1989–95

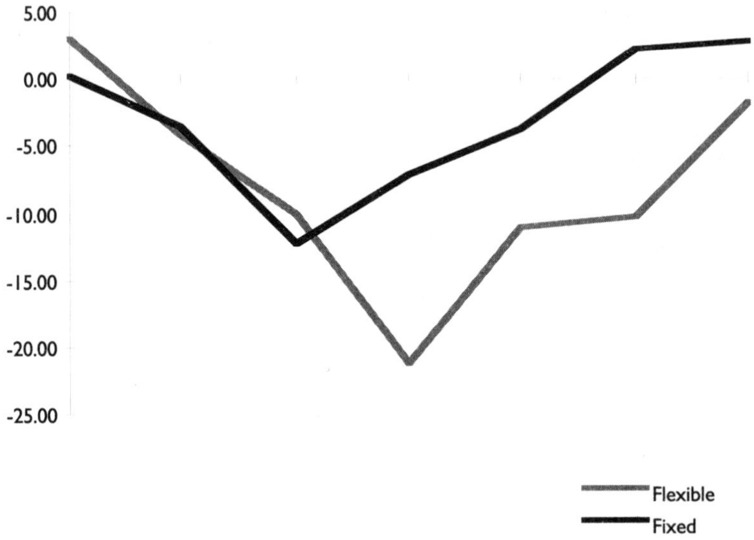

Flexible
Fixed

Source: EBRD (1995–96)

observed in transition economies. Indeed, output collapsed at the outset of all stabilization programs—except in Hungary in 1990—irrespective of the type of program adopted. During the first year of stabilization, output fell by 18.6 percent in countries that chose flexible exchange rates and by 11.8 percent in countries that opted for fixed exchange rates (figure 1.3). It should also be noted that wage policy featured in all programs in transition economies. Thus, it is impossible for one to distinguish so-called orthodox from heterodox programs.[4]

2.2.1 Fixed versus Flexible Exchange Rates

Countries that adopted flexible exchange rates display inflation rates that are higher initially and more persistent over time. Thus, experience shows that the lack of an exchange rate anchor makes it difficult to stabilize inflation. However, the time dimension of the relationship between the exchange rate regime and inflation has to be taken into account. Indeed, it may be misleading to conclude that flexible rates imply a higher initial burst of inflation

16

(Wyplosz 1995). The initial jump in the price level seems to be closely associated with the ex ante macroeconomic disequilibria, especially the prereform monetary overhang (see Calvo and Coricelli 1994). These ex ante disequilibria generally led to balance-of-payments deficits and a hemorrhage of international reserves. Thus, countries suffering from these problems began reforms without the cushion of international reserves needed to defend the peg initially. The causality seems to go from underlying inflationary pressures to the choice of the exchange rate regime, and not vice versa.

Less ambiguous is the observation that inflation tends to be persistently higher in the floating rate countries. Fiscal deficits were much larger in floating rate countries (Wyplosz 1995). With deficits on the order of 10 percent of GDP, entirely financed by money creation, fixed exchange rates could hardly be sustained. Thus, the need for a larger inflation compelled several countries to switch to a more flexible exchange rate regime. Nevertheless,

Figure 1.4

Exchange Rate Regime and Budget Deficits

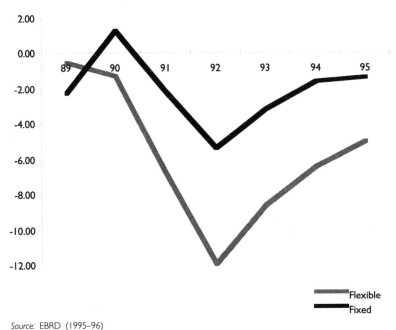

Source: EBRD (1995–96)

17

in the successful experiences of stabilization with flexible exchange rates (Slovenia and Latvia), there was a large fiscal adjustment. Some observers argued that by adopting fixed exchange rates these countries could have done even better (Sahay and Végh 1996). However, there is no evidence that fixed rates exerted a disciplining effect on budget deficits. Budget deficits actually increased after the first year of reforms in several ERBs (Poland and Hungary, for instance). Figure 1.4 shows that ERBs display a worsening of the budget in the two years after launching the programs, while flexible exchange rate programs display an improvement of the budget after stabilization, although the level of the budget remains higher than in ERBs.[5] Moreover, in some instances fixed exchange regimes were abandoned rather quickly, as the case of Poland testifies.

For those countries of the fSU that after three to four years from the start of liberalization are still trying to stabilize inflation, the choice of the exchange rate regime is still an open question. The case for adopting the exchange rate anchor seems strong in these cases. One fundamental argument in favor of the exchange rate anchor for these countries is that the period of high inflation has led to a flight from domestic currency. Foreign currency deposits for which data are available increased sharply in such countries as Russia and Ukraine.[6] In Ukraine, for instance, foreign currency deposits as a share of broad money grew from 16 percent in 1992 to 56 percent in 1994. In such a context, domestic money supply may be a highly inefficient instrument for controlling inflation.

However, the experience with fixed exchange rates, even in transition economies, has shown the difficulties in sustaining a system of rigidly fixed exchange rates. The real appreciation of the exchange rate that has invariably accompanied these experiences has induced some countries to adopt more flexible exchange rate policies. Poland moved in late 1991 to a crawling peg; Hungary adopted a crawling band at the end of 1994; the Czech Republic adopted a similar system in 1995. These changes were affected as well by recent large inflows of foreign capital to the above three countries (see Calvo, Sahay, and Végh 1994).

2.2.2 Real Effects of Different Programs and the Nature of the Output Collapse

The fact that the implementation of these programs coincided with fundamental shocks to trading relations, such as the arrangement established by the Council for Mutual Economic Assistance (CMEA), complicates the evaluation of the real effects of stabilization-cum-reform programs. Although we are still lacking a fully convincing account, both analytical and empirical, of the effects of the demise of the CMEA, most studies show the relevance of such demise for the output decline of Central and Eastern European countries. As countries were affected by different exposure to such shock, because of different weights of CMEA trade, as well as different implicit subsidies involved in the arrangement, the real effects of the demise of the CMEA were likely heterogeneous (see Rodrik 1993).

The general view is that the demise of the CMEA represents an exogenous shock to output, with demand side and supply side implications (terms-of-trade effect). However, a closer look at the issue suggests that the demise of the CMEA can be interpreted as a sudden international credit shock, with the destruction of a centralized payment system.

Furthermore, the CMEA shock was asymmetric. While the shock was negative for countries subsidized by the CMEA, it was positive for countries—such as Russia—that were implicitly taxed. However, the output decline was even larger in Russia than in the countries of Central and Eastern Europe heavily subsidized under the CMEA. Thus, the CMEA shock cannot be a general explanation for the output decline in transition economies.

The dynamic path, or cycle, of ERBs in Latin America and Israel (Kiguel and Liviatan 1991) has not been observed in transition economies. As suggested by Aldes, Kiguel, and Liviatan (1995), both ERBs and MBs relied on tight credit policy. In the short run, the latter probably dominated the possible positive effects on output brought about by exchange-rate-based stabilization programs. Indeed, Aldes, Kiguel, and Liviatan suggest that even in market economies a main reason for ERBs to lead to an initial contraction of output is tight credit.[7]

With these caveats in mind, one can nevertheless observe that measures of the real costs of different stabilization programs offer ambiguous results. Indeed, GDP fell more in floaters, while

19

Figure 1.5

Exchange Rate Regime and Unemployment

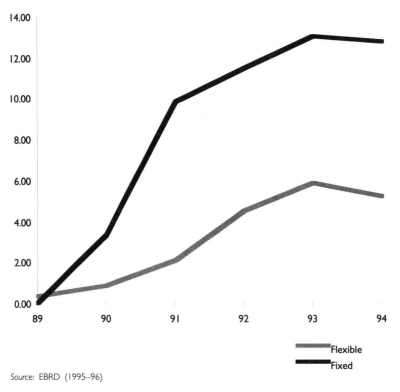

Source: EBRD (1995–96)

employment fell less—and unemployment grew less (figure 1.5). Some observers have argued that fixed exchange rate programs were successful in reining in inflation, but at higher costs, measuring the real cost in terms of employment decline (Wyplosz 1995). However, as will be argued in chapter 3, employment and unemployment changes cannot be interpreted merely as indicators of the costs of reform, as they are also indicators of restructuring.

In sum, from the impressionistic evidence discussed one could conclude that inflation can be stabilized even in countries with very rigid economic structures (Sahay and Végh 1996), irrespective of the nominal anchors chosen. However, a closer look at the evidence indicates that stabilizing inflation has been very hard—in fact in some cases a failure—in countries characterized by very rigid structures and large macroeconomic imbalances (for example, in the fSU).

Thus, irrespective of the type of stabilization program and the exposure to the CMEA shock, output fell sharply in all stabilization programs. Moreover, the output decline took place at the start of stabilization. In some cases (for example, Poland), the decline was sudden and concentrated in the first few months of the program. These features led several observers to describe the output decline as a phenomenon of "trade implosion" (Calvo and Coricelli 1993; Kornai 1993). This suggests that the output collapse reflects the sudden disruption of old coordination mechanisms. This interpretation emphasizes the importance of the interaction between macroeconomic policies and systemic factors.

2.2.2.1 Trade Implosion

Disruption of coordination mechanisms can be considered a source of supply-side bottlenecks. Supply-side disruptions likely played a role, especially in the most rigidly centralized economies. However, their quantitative importance is uncertain. Even the most obvious examples of anticipated disruptions associated with the old structure of production, namely the military industry, ended up being less important compared to the aggregate collapse in output.

Perhaps the clearest example of supply-side disruptions was associated with the decentralization of vertically integrated economies. Indeed, the higher the degree of central intervention in ensuring the production process, the larger the supply shock (which seems to be confirmed by survey data reported in Blanchard 1996). This aspect has a domestic and an international dimension (the demise of the CMEA). In those cases in which economic decentralization preceded radical reforms (as in Hungary and Poland), supply bottlenecks seem to have played a minor role. In these cases, we will argue, credit more than supply bottlenecks was the main source of disruption of coordination mechanisms.

It is conceivable that the breakup of old coordination mechanisms could directly lead to a fall in output. One channel would be the appearance of alternatives to selling to old customers (Blanchard 1996). Sellers would thus have a reservation price, below which no sale takes place. The buyer may offer a price below the reservation price, with the result of a fall in output.

Blanchard asks the obvious question of why state firms do not offer higher prices to their suppliers. His answer is that the firm does not know which supplier has true alternative customers. A simpler explanation is that state firms simply cannot afford to pay for these inputs at the higher price, as they are liquidity constrained. We elaborate this explanation in chapter 2.

One can also envision a different channel, possibly relevant in countries in which hoarding goods is still attractive for firms, because of negative real interest rates on financial savings. Before reforms, hunger for hoarding was somehow curtailed by the imposition of the plan. After reforms, firms were free to choose their level of inventories. Hoarding of inputs may create serious bottlenecks in the production process, with a consequent fall in output. This channel was probably relevant in countries implementing partial reforms (fSU). It could also have worked in countries unable to stabilize inflation. Indeed, there is some evidence that production of finished goods fell more than production of inputs in countries of the fSU.

The trade implosion view predicts a fall in productivity, together with the fall in output. This is an important phenomenon that is hardly explained by transition models based on "creative destruction." These models may account for the aggregate fall in output, but they generally imply increasing productivity (see Kehoe 1995). Consider a simple two-sector model with an expanding, more productive private sector and a declining, less productive state sector. The private sector pulls labor away from state firms. During the transition some of the workers laid off from the state sector remain unemployed. Thus, aggregate output declines initially. However, labor productivity increases in the declining state sector, as labor shedding takes place.

3. Liberalization and Stabilization: Pitfalls of Macroeconomic Policies in Transition Economies

The above discussion pointed out a few important peculiarities of the experience of transition economies. A key distinctive feature is that stabilization was often launched simultaneously with price liberalization.

Liberalization is undoubtedly a key component of the reform strategies. Price liberalization and opening of foreign trade proceeded rapidly in most transition countries. The implications of price liberalization had at least two dimensions. One, of a micro-economic or sectoral nature, is that the price system in the previous regime implied a large redistribution of resources across sectors through taxes and subsidies. Price liberalization meant the elimination of these taxes and subsidies. The other dimension is of a macroeconomic nature and is related to the so-called monetary overhang. In the absence of a complete set of unofficial markets, price controls led in most countries to a significant imbalance between desired and actual monetary incomes. At the going prices, consumers would have consumed more goods, if available in the market. Thus, consumers were rationed, and shortages often characterized centrally planned economies. Under conditions of monetary overhang, price liberalization can lead to a price-level jump and even to an initial overshooting of the price-level. The difficulty of distinguishing levels and rates of change—a theme that will recur in this book—and the perception by policymakers of the risks of translating a price-level increase into a sustained inflation rate, prompted stabilization programs that in many cases set their instruments as if the price level jump were a jump in the rate of inflation. In fact, the uncertainty facing policymakers went well beyond the difficulty of forecasting underlying inflationary pressures. The uncertainty involved the characteristics of firms—their viability—and, finally, the response of economic actors to new incentives and rules of the game.

3.1 Designing Policies in Conditions of Uncertainty

Policymakers face three main sets of uncertainties. First, there is uncertainty about the magnitude of the monetary overhang accumulated in the previous regime. Second, a large share of enterprises might well be unviable in the new system of free prices. Third, there is a fundamental uncertainty about the effects of various untested instruments of economic policy. We focus on the first two types of uncertainty.

3.1.1 Uncertainty about the Size of the Ex Ante Monetary Overhang

The uncertainty regarding the underlying inflationary pressures is clearly revealed by the large gap between forecast and actual inflation after price liberalization (Calvo and Coricelli 1993). Although this is a feature common to most IMF-supported stabilization programs, the magnitude of the forecast error for economies in transition is striking. If one assumes that the monetary overhang was positively correlated with the measured ratio between broad money and output, one should expect the post-reform price jump to be linked to the prereform inverse-velocity of money (Calvo and Coricelli 1994).

The fact that the initial increase in prices was much larger than expected may be an indication of the uncertainty surrounding the design of stabilization programs in these countries. The explanation should be somewhat different depending on the type of exchange rate regime adopted. With fixed exchange rates, the initial price-level jump largely depended on the size of the initial devaluation (see Bruno 1993; Halpern and Wyplosz 1995). However, even in countries that adopted flexible exchange rates, the initial price jump had a largely exogenous component, as a key aspect of price liberalization was the increase in the price of energy, a controlled price. In addition to what can be described as forecast error due to ignorance of the underlying structure of the economy, there was likely an error due to difficulties in predicting the behavior of economic actors.[8] The high degree of concentration of production and trade was considered a main threat to price stability. Opening the economy to foreign competition played a major role in limiting monopolistic power, especially in smaller economies. In larger and less open economies, the presence of monopolies was considered a justification for maintaining some form of price regulation (for instance, maximum markup over costs, in the case of Russia).

In addition to monopolistic power, one important fact is that the further price setters were from the consumer market, the higher the increase in prices. This phenomenon is apparent from the large gap between producer and consumer prices at the outset of several liberalization programs (in Poland and Russia, for instance). Besides differences in the weights of various goods in the two indices, one possible explanation for this gap is the lack of market discipline in transactions among enterprises (see McKinnon 1993). Calvo and Coricelli (1994) provide a simple analytical discussion of this phenomenon, showing that the limited use of money in interenterprise transactions and default on payments due may lead to prices higher than those that will emerge if money were used to effect interenterprise exchanges.

3.1.2 Price Jump, Stocks, and Flows

One source of such psychology is the monetarist habit of defining monetary policy by growth rates of aggregates. This leads to undiscriminating extrapolation of currently announced targets for one quarter or one year or of deviations from targets. In the United States, Chairman Volker needs to convince his nervous financial constituency that the economy needs and can safely absorb a change in the level of money stock, and that this by no means signifies permanently higher rates of growth.

James Tobin

If the initial jump in prices was partly exogenous, setting nominal targets for the stock of money implied a certain stock of real monetary balances. In terms of macroeconomic policies this raises the well-known issue of stocks and flows in stabilization programs. However, this issue takes on a peculiar relevance in economies in transition. Focusing, for the sake of argument, only on the monetary aspect of stabilization, it is easy to show that *unless nominal prices are downward flexible,* the unanticipated switch from a higher to a lower rate of inflation, and thus the rate of money creation, requires an initial upward adjustment in the stock of money at the date of stabilization (Sargent 1982). This follows from a simple arithmetic arising when money demand is a decreasing function of expected inflation. Suppose the economy is traveling along a path in which inflation equals the rate of growth of money, say μ. At the time of stabilization, the rate of growth of money is reduced to zero. From that point onwards, inflation and expected inflation will be equal to zero. However, at the time of implementation of the new policy, demand for the stock of money, say at time t, is equal to

$$M_t - P_t = -\gamma \, (E_t P_{t+1} - P_t) + Y_t, \text{ with } \gamma > 0 \tag{1}$$

If expected inflation drops, the right-hand side of the equation increases and thus the left-hand side should also increase. If the price level cannot decline, this can be achieved only through a once-and-for-all increase in the nominal stock of money. Otherwise, equilibrium in the money market can be achieved only through a contraction in real output. Although this conflict between stocks and flows has a general applicability (see the quotation from Tobin at the beginning of this section) it is particularly important in the context of transition economies.

The reason is apparent from equation (1) if one notes that at time t, reforming countries reduced the rate of growth of money, but at the same time implemented measures that pushed up the price level P_t. Thus, the required upward shift in the stock of money might have been very large for economies in transition. Accordingly, there was a justified fear that such an initial adjustment could have been interpreted as a signal of a permanently higher rate of growth of money supply. However, there are two main arguments against such an approach. First, the price level jumped up anyway. Even though the initial jump could have been larger in the presence of a more accommodative stance regarding monetary policy, if people confuse levels with rates of changes in money stocks, they would also confuse level with rates of changes in prices. Second, several programs adopted the exchange rate anchor, and thus the excessive tightening of monetary policy somehow contradicted the same rationale for implementing such types of programs.[9]

In a paper with Roberto Rocha (Coricelli and Rocha 1991), we advanced the view that price liberalization could be effected before launching stabilization programs. The argument was based on evidence from the Yugoslav program of January 1990, whereby price liberalization, accommodated by a blip in money supply, was carried out before launching the ERB program. The period of adjustment was short, to avoid runaway inflation. The program was very successful in the first few months. Inflation dropped almost instantaneously to zero and the output fall was moderate. Later in 1990 political pressure led to the failure of the program.

Thus, even though there are strong reasons for implementing ERBs in economies in transition, the timing and the accompanying measures at the time of launching the programs were probably wrong. As stressed above, given the size of the needed adjustment in the price level and in relative prices, price liberalization could have preceded the launching of the stabilization program. Furthermore, the sharp devaluation of the exchange rate that was effected with the adoption of the fixed peg was ill conceived. Indeed, as shown by Halpern and Wyplosz (1995), the initial devaluation was generally excessive, fueling inflation and subsequent appreciation of the real exchange rate. In fact, the sharp fall in real monetary balances could have been averted or softened by a stable nominal exchange rate or even by an appreciation. In the case of Poland, inflation persisted at high levels after stabilization, despite a surplus in the budget balance.

In sum, the initial stock of credit could be adjusted (at least to the expected new price level). Regarding interest rate policy, probably more relevant in several cases than the quantity constraints, the interest rate should be set in relation to expected inflation after the initial price jump.[10] Indeed, the former Czechoslovakia followed this rule in 1991, while Poland in 1990 followed a rather extreme approach by trying to set the nominal interest rate in line with the initial inflation (the price jump) (see Calvo and Coricelli 1993).

Despite these drawbacks to the programs implemented, justification for initial tight money may arise from microeconomic rather than macroeconomic considerations. One manifestation of the so-called soft budget constraint in the centrally planned regime was the passive role of credit and money. Credit did not constrain enterprise decisions. Tightening of monetary policy signaled a break with the fully accommodative stance of the prereform regime. The disciplining role of credit policy is a fundamental aspect of the analysis of the experience of PCPEs. Chapter 2 is devoted to this issue, and there we argue against this view. The next section discusses possible shortcomings of a policy of across-the-board credit contraction in a context of high uncertainty about the viability of firms.

3.2 Uncertainty about the Share of Nonviable Firms and Endogeneity of Policy Credibility

Although there is still confusion over the exact meaning of *nonviable firms* in the context of a radically changing economic regime, the problem of nonviable firms has been at the center of the debate on reforms in PCPEs. Centrally planned economies were characterized by an arbitrary structure of production. Even firms with negative value added could survive by receiving subsidies. Estimates of the share of negative value added production varied across countries. However, even for the supposedly better positioned economies of Central and Eastern Europe, such estimates ranged between 20 and 30 percent of total industrial production.[11] Note that these estimates do not measure the likely reallocation of resources across sectors. Indeed, there are activities that yield positive value added but produce returns on the capital invested that are well below market returns. Thus, resources would move from these sectors to the more remunerative activities. The negative value added activities indicate the pressure, in the short run, on output and employment. Indeed, the government would be better off, even from a budgetary point of view, if it could shut down these activities and pay wages to the workers employed.[12] The problem, however, is that the government cannot identify the activities that should be shut down. Parameters from the old regime are not a good guide for predicting viability in the new market regime. Indeed, low productivity levels in the old regime could originate from lack of key inputs, obsolete capital stock, and shirking of the labor force. Thus, an initial investment in restructuring the capital stock, in addition to an improvement in the incentives, could make viable even firms showing negative value added. With perfect capital markets, these firms could borrow to finance the initial restructuring costs; however, it is likely that the information problems affect the financial sector as well (see chapter 2). Indeed, the latter is initially just the financial branch of the government.

With imperfect financial markets, firms may lack the needed resources for restructuring and may thus collapse under the new regime. Thus, there is a genuine policy decision for the government to make on the speed at which subsidies should be eliminated and on the amount and distribution of credit to be provided. In chapter 2 we discuss "structural" reasons that can make undesirable a big-bang approach. Here we emphasize a channel that works through the endogenous weakening of the credibility of a big-bang program.

An important complication to the introduction of hard budget constraints is that they may lead to such a large temporary drop in economic activity that the drop itself may jeopardize the credibility of the hard budget constraints. Especially in a context of regime change, with no reputation built by the new governments, credibility is likely to be largely endogenous. For this endogeneity to arise, it is sufficient to assume that the government will not maintain the announced policies if the economic conditions are particularly bad. Thus, the government will likely change its policy if economic conditions are worse than a given tolerance level. The condition for such endogeneity is even weaker, as it is sufficient that the public expects the government to change the policy in a particularly unfavourable situation.

4. Liberalization and Speed of Transition: Reform Measures and Initial Conditions

The preceding sections have shown that developments in economies in transition cannot be understood within simple short-run macroeconomic models. One should therefore evaluate the interplay of institutional reforms, macroeconomic policies, and macroeconomic performance. Within the areas of institutional and structural reforms are fundamental issues regarding the speed of transformation of the economy. Several countries have accumulated a postreform experience of six to seven years. The initial recession has given way to a recovery, in some cases very strong. For the countries of the fSU, the postreform experience is shorter. Nevertheless, cross-country analysis may help to evaluate even the experience of these countries as the first stage of a medium-term transition phase.

Leaving aside non-European countries, twenty-six countries are engaged in the transition from centrally planned to market economies in the 1990s. The large number of countries makes a

Figure 1.6

Initial Liberalization and Output Decline

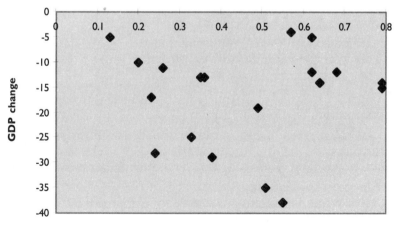

Source: EBRD (1995–96)

29

Figure 1.6a

Initial Liberalization and Output Fall

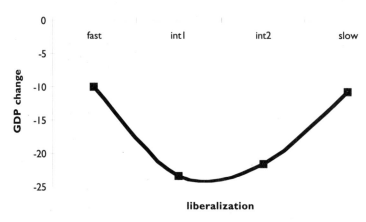

Source: EBRD (1995–96)

cross-country analysis particularly complex. To highlight some reg-ularities it is useful to create subgroups of countries. We shall con-sider the classifications created by the EBRD and by the World Bank. These indicators try to capture the stage of transition reached by the various countries. Such a division is inevitably arbi-trary. One problem of the EBRD indicators, however, is that they do not measure the speed of transition, an important concept in the analytical framework underpinning this book. Therefore, we also use year-by-year indicators constructed by the World Bank.

We shall begin by stressing five main facts:

(1.) Initially, faster liberalization translated into a greater fall in output (figures 1.6 and 1.6a).

(2.) The relationship between speed of reform and output performance is highly nonlinear (figure 1. 7): very fast and very slow reform both lead to better outcomes than a middle-ground speed.

(3.) While cumulative reforms appear positively correlated with output performance, there seems to be an even stronger cor-relation between favorable initial conditions, in terms of pre-

Figure 1.7

Liberalization and Growth, 1990–94

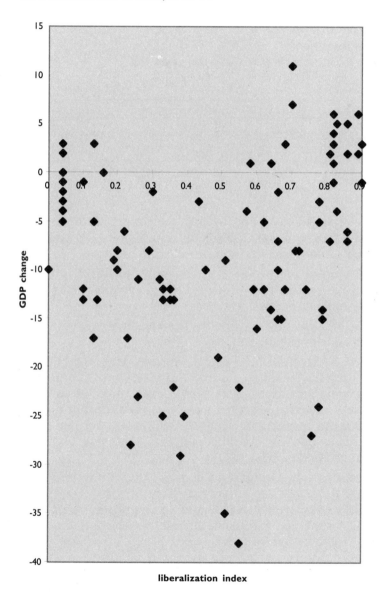

Source: EBRD (1995–96)

Table 1.2

Private Sector Development and Output Changes, 1989–94

Sample: 26 countries
OLS regression
Dependent variable: Percentage changes in GDP

Variable	Coefficient	t-statistics
Constant	-81.42	-5.60
Private*	-225.06	-4.99
Private squared	80.98	5.06
R-squared	0.30	

*Private: World Bank indicator of private sector development (see De Melo et al. 1996)

reform liberalization, and postreform output performance. Thus, it is not easy to disentangle the role of reforms from those of favorable initial conditions.

(4.) Output performance seems to be positively correlated with private sector development, although the relationship again appears nonlinear (table 1.2).

(5.) Inflation has remained relatively high even in the successful countries (figure 1.8).

These facts raise three main questions. First, why did faster liberalization lead to a larger initial output decline? The analysis of the preceding section suggests that liberalization per se was not the cause—or perhaps not the main cause—of output decline. It was rather the combination of liberalization and excessively tight constraints, especially credit constraints, that may explain the trade implosion observed initially.

Second, if initial conditions appear to be so important, what aspects of the initial conditions that were crucial (macrostability, minimum market structure, degree of openness, etc.)? In this regard, we argue that a minimum market structure (including the size of the private sector at the outset of reforms) likely played a crucial role. Alternatively, countries starting from an industrial structure more in line with comparative advantages (as in the Czech Republic) were subject to smaller reallocation shocks, and thus smaller adjustment costs.

Figure 1.8

Poland: Inflation Poststabilization, 1991–95

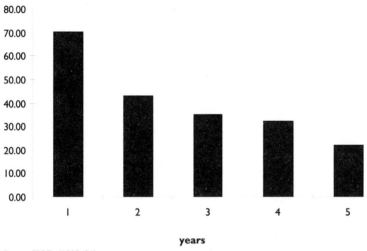

years

Source: EBRD (1995–96)

As to the effects of liberalization, there is a prima facie strong correlation between liberalization and better economic performance (Sachs 1996). Taking the period 1989–94 (or 1989–95), it turns out that average GDP growth is positively correlated with the degree of liberalization. However, the relationship between liberalization and growth is nonlinear. De Melo, Denizer, and Gelb (1996) address this nonlinearity by defining a threshold level for the index of liberalization. They show that the longer countries stay below that threshold, the worse their performance is relative to the faster reformers. Nevertheless, the model predicts that during the first two postreform years, fast reformers are outperformed by slow reformers in terms of both output growth and inflation. However, as the starting dates of reforms differ across countries, there are no overlapping samples of fast and slow reformers in the period under study. Therefore, there is no ultimate evidence for the benefits of different strategies. In fact, Fischer, Sahay, and Végh (1996) find that, after correcting for different starting dates, the performance of different countries is more homogeneous than generally believed.[13]

33

Table 1.3

Regression on Output 1993–94 with Respect to 1989 and Liberalization Indices

	Coefficients	t-stat	Coefficients	t-stat
Constant	53.60	10.60	69.40	8.20
Cumulative liberalization	9.60	2.50	-2.70	-0.70
Dummy for War	-28.60	-2.70	-35.60	-4.70
Prereform liberalization			124.70	4.70
Observations	28.00		28.00	
R^2	0.33		0.37	

Despite the insights gained from these analyses, a fundamental confusion remains about how to interpret several results. The existing literature does not tackle three main aspects. First, there is the usual causality problem. Even if one accepts the association between better performance and bolder reform strategy, it is not obvious that causality goes from reforms to performance and not vice versa. Indeed, it could be argued that only in countries affected by more favorable conditions (less severe exogenous shocks or less severe "inherited shocks") can a bolder reform strategy be sustained. Second, to evaluate the independent role of different reform strategies, one must control for different initial conditions.[14] Third, given the simultaneous occurrence of several reform measures, it is hard to disentangle the independent role of certain measures relative to others. This issue opens the important question of the complementarity of different reform measures (Friedman and Johnson 1995). It is not easy to address the three issues empirically. Nevertheless, available data do permit the analysis of the relative roles of reform strategies—speed and breadth of liberalization measures—and initial conditions.

5.1 Initial Conditions versus Reform Strategies

Using the data set put together by the World Bank, table 1.3 illustrates the importance of initial conditions. The regression links the cumulative output performance during the period 1989-94 to cumulative liberalization, initial level of the liberalization index, and a dummy for countries affected by war. What is remarkable is that the impact of the index of liberalization becomes statistically insignificant when the indicator of initial conditions in terms of liberalization is included. Of course, there are many aspects of initial conditions that are not captured by the prereform liberalization indicator. Initial macroeconomic disequilibria and structural distortions are likely to be important determinants of subsequent economic performance. However, the prereform liberalization index is a good proxy of the extent of development of markets and of private sector activities. The index mainly reflects the occurrence of partial reforms within the old regime. Interestingly, these partial reforms, meant to improve the efficiency of the planned economy, failed to achieve their primary objectives but created the seeds for a better performance during the period of market reforms.

The importance of initial conditions suggests that the postreform dynamics can be best characterized in terms of multiple equilibria. The correlation between transition indicators and performance should be seen as a two-way relationship within a complex and dynamic framework. Similar policies can be associated with totally different outcomes if initial conditions are different. Countries can get stuck in inefficient equilibria. In these cases transition will not proceed further, or at least it will be subject to a significant slowdown. The relationship between transition indicators and performance should be interpreted as going from performance to transition.

We shall discuss several examples of this direction of causality. It is useful, however, to state at the outset that it is crucial to cast the analysis of transition in a dynamic context. Indeed, transition is a genuinely dynamic process, characterized by highly non-linear phenomena. Reforms face an intertemporal trade-off due to the distortions or imperfections present in the market system, which reforms try to tackle. In a perfect market system, the same idea of reform is meaningless. With imperfect markets—we will try to be more precise in the sequel about what we mean by imperfections—reform policies that may enhance efficiency in the medium run are likely to lead to short-term losses. Furthermore, the larger the initial imperfections, the larger the initial costs. Thus, there may be a hump at the beginning of transition. Successful reforms have to go beyond the hump. Depending on the initial conditions, however, policies consistent with long-run efficiency may adversely affect or even determine a reversal of the reform process. Another important aspect of the dynamic process is that the economy can adapt over time to the new market conditions. Ex post, good performance can be observed, although this has little to do with the initial therapy.[15]

6. Summing Up: Lessons for Macroeconomic Policies

Overall, although the magnitude of the initial output collapse cannot be ascribed mainly to macroeconomic policies, it seems that the design of macroeconomic policies contributed to such a decline. In this respect, three main points stand out from the above analysis.

First, price liberalization can be effected in one step, and there are several advantages in doing that. However, it is probably advisable to complete price liberalization before introducing severe constraints on the amount of credit available in the economy. Indeed, price liberalization implies large changes in relative prices. Imposing tight constraints on credit may actually produce results that conflict with the needed reallocation of resources among firms and sectors.

Second, the fundamental distinction between stocks and flows and levels and rates of change of variables has been generally overlooked by policymakers and advisors. Such a distinction has important policy implications. To begin with, price liberalization can be effected with flexible exchange rates. The exchange rate will be fixed after having completed the "corrective" price adjustment. Fixing the exchange rate and starting out with a large depreciation (with a voluntary overshooting) has serious shortcomings (see Coricelli, De la Calle, and Pinto 1990). As noted above, it may lead to a credit crunch (contractionary devaluation). Moreover, it leaves room for persistent inflation as the adjustment to the new world prices may be gradual. In addition, credit policy must take into account that the initial price jump is an increase in the price level, not in the rate of inflation.

Third, initial conditions, especially in terms of the presence of a minimum structure of market institutions and behaviors, played a key role. Policies should take these initial conditions into account. The crucial role of initial conditions suggests that reforms can lead to multiple equilibria.

2

Monetary Policy and Financial Markets in Transition Economies

1. Introduction

This chapter emphasizes the crucial role of financial markets in the operation of economies whose initial conditions were characterized by developed industrial structures and completely underdeveloped financial markets. Several types of equilibria with respect to financial structures can emerge from reforms. A main hypothesis is that the underdevelopment of financial markets implies a crucial role for liquidity in determining output in these economies. Prereform industrial structures were rigid, with interfirm linkages hard to change in the short run. In extreme cases, the whole economy was functioning as a unique, vertically integrated sector. Monetary exchanges and credit contracts were irrelevant to the operation of the system. Since reforms have gotten underway, interfirm exchanges take place through monetary transfers, either payments on delivery or delayed payments (trade credit). In a developed industrial structure most firms are both suppliers and customers of other firms. The higher the degree of "circularity" of the system, the higher the exposure of the system will be to local shocks. Financial difficulties of one firm can be transmitted to the entire system through the chain that links the firms. A key question to analyze is what happened when bank credit was sharply restricted at the outset of reforms. In "normal" circumstances, the withdrawal of the central bank as *lender of last resort* should have increased the risk in any credit market, including trade credit. All sources of credit should have contracted, creating serious financial difficulties for firms. However, the experience has been heterogeneous across countries. In some countries, the contraction of bank credit was accompanied by the blossoming of interenterprise arrears. While these arrears may have softened the initial crunch, they entailed large social costs. Arrears are different from voluntary trade credit, and in fact they can hamper the development of an efficient trade credit market. In other transition countries, such as Poland, interenterprise credit fell together with bank credit.[1]

The liquidity aspect of credit-monetary policy in PCPEs has been largely understated. More attention has been devoted to the disciplining role of credit markets. However, the liquidity and discipline aspects of credit policy cannot be separated. Indeed, both loose and excessively tight credit policies can lead to negative effects on output as well as on "market discipline." Excessive tightening of credit policy may lead to generalized default and consequent lack of discipline, followed by a loosening of policy to avoid a financial collapse. Such a situation is analogous to the progressive "demonetization" of an economy determined by runaway inflation within the context of an automatically accommodative monetary policy.

The response of the economy to the sudden credit/monetary tightening depends on the initial conditions of the economy in terms of economic structure and institutional development. Particularly important is the role played by private trade credit markets in response to the break-up of the traditional automatic financing operated by the banks. Note that in economic history bank credit followed the development of trade credit. Centralization of credit created out of the seeds of the decentralized credit arrangements developed by individual traders. The experience of economies in transition reversed such a sequence. Under central planning, trade credit was generally forbidden by law. With market reforms, the highly centralized credit is suddenly frozen, and firms are left to their own initiative to regulate their transactions and credit arrangements. Not surprisingly, the functioning of private credit markets crucially depends on a minimum market structure that imposes credible penalties for "bad" behavior and rewards for "good" behavior. In this respect, these countries started from highly heterogenous initial conditions which, we argue, had a decisive impact on the effects of similar macroeconomic policies applied to different countries.

The next sections present a simple analytical structure to assess the different paths an economy can follow after the introduction of market reforms. We start with a brief introduction to the workings of the monetary system in the prereform regime.

2. Transition from Central Planning to a Market Economy

The prereform period was characterized by a system of a fully accommodating financial sector. There were no financial constraints on economic activity. Both bad and good projects were financed; thus, the financial sector did not provide an effective selection mechanism. This form of accommodation was one of the forms of the so-called soft budget constraint.

To interrupt this automatic lending was one of the main objectives at the outset of reforms. Given the underdevelopment of the banking system, this coincided with an across-the-board cut in credit. Is there any evidence that within such a contraction, there was also a positive reallocation of credit away from the inefficient firms? In fact, both theory and empirical evidence tend to indicate that there was a high degree of inertia.

The simple model used in this chapter implies that good firms could accumulate their funds and thus recover, relative to the bad firms. Thus, there will be a process of "disintermediation" of banks with respect to financing good firms. Nevertheless, the economy can recover after the initial contraction. This has often been interpreted as a positive outcome of "imposing hard budget constraints." However, the role of the financial sector is not to starve firms of funds indiscriminately, but to support an efficient reallocation of resources across firms and sectors. One aspect of such function is that of allowing viable firms to overcome the inefficiencies of strict cash constraints. Self-financing has serious drawbacks. First, self-financing of working capital dries out cash-flow for investment. Second, a system working on cash payments requires the maintenance of large inventories of money and/or goods to insure against possible shortfalls in future money receipts. Third, default by bad firms puts strain on banks. Fourth, trade credit markets may be adversely affected by the cut in bank credit. The increased default in trade credit markets may provoke a movement towards cash payments. Even more serious is the risk that generalized default pushes the economy into a low-output equilibrium, either because of the persistence—as an "equilibrium" phenomenon—of the default regime, or because of pressure on the government to abandon stabilization. Both outcomes were observed in actual experience, for instance, in Romania, Russia, and Ukraine.

3. A Simple Analytical Model

Let us begin with a brief discussion of a highly stylized model of the prereform period (see Garvy 1996 for a more detailed analysis).

3.1 Prereform Period

We assume the economy is populated by two types of firms, one producing inputs, using only labor, and the other producing a finished product, using labor and the input obtained from the other sector.

3.1.1 Output-Good Firms

Bank credit finances the purchase of inputs. At the beginning of period t, firms purchase a stock of inputs n_t, which is used during period t. For simplicity, we focus on a case with no inventories. Output is produced with a regular production function, with labor as a fixed factor:

$$y_t = f(n_t) \tag{1}$$

Assuming money as the numeraire, and with t denoting taxes, net revenues in terms of money of firm o are

$$P_t^o y_t - W_t^o - t_t = M_t^o - M_{t-1}^o \tag{2}$$

Net revenues are deposited in the monobank. Inputs are purchased using bank credit; thus,

$$P_t^i n_t = BC_t \tag{3}$$

Wages are paid at the end of the period.

3.1.2 Input-Good Firms

Input goods are produced using only labor as a variable factor:

$$n_t = g(L_t^i) \tag{4}$$

A wage fund is allocated by the bank to the firm to pay wages at the end of period t:

$$W_t^i = M_t^i \tag{5}$$

Although wages do not affect the liquidity constraint at time t, they are crucial in affecting available cash over time, as profits determine the cash flow of the firm. Demand for final (consumption) goods is assumed to be a function of total wages, for simplicity a constant fraction of total wages:

$$\beta(W_t^o + W_t^i) = P_t^o y_t \tag{6}$$

The timing structure implicit in this setting implies that wages are paid simultaneously to household consumption. Domestic money is the only form in which household savings can be kept; thus,

$$(1 - \beta)(W_t^o + W_t^i) = M_t^h - M_{t-1}^h \tag{7}$$

Assuming that the plan works effectively, in each period bank deposits of output-good firms should equal credit received. Money deposited by output-good firms covers the wage fund for the input-good firms:

$$M_t^o = BC_t = M_t^i \tag{8}$$

Both types of firms break even, and they do not accumulate money over time. It is apparent that outside money is needed to pay wages. Given the specific timing of transactions that we assumed, the government needs to issue money for only a proportion of total wages, namely, wages in the input-good sector.

Substituting the demand equation into the household savings function, and using the fact that deposits of the output-good firms equal their loans, and that wages in the input-good sector correspond to the wage fund made available to them by the commercial bank (or the commercial branch of the monobank), we obtain:

$$M2_t - M2_{t-1} = M_t^i - M_{t-1}^i + (1-\beta)(W_t^o + W_t^i) \qquad (9)$$
$$= W_t^i - W_{t-1}^i + (1-\beta)2W_t^i$$

where we assumed that $W^i = W^o$. When $\beta=1$, the change in broad money equals the change in wages (and in base money). However, if $\beta<1$, broad money grows even when wages remain constant.

From the above equations we can compute the price levels that ensure goods market equilibrium for given real output and wages. Equilibrium between demand and supply of consumption goods implies

$$b(W_t^o + W_t^i) = P_t^o y_t \qquad (10)$$

As outside money equals the wage fund in the input-good sector, and money is finally held by households, the constant stock of outside money equals

$$M_t^i = M_t^h = \overline{M} \qquad (11)$$

In this system, the planner fixes both prices and output. In the economy as a whole wages are constrained by total GDP. Money is totally endogenous. However, if the plan is well executed and all firms break even, money is constant over time. Base money is thus equal to $\overline{M}$. $M2$ is equal to $2\overline{M}$, or $2W^i$. Note that GDP is equal to $W^i + W^o$. Velocity of M2 is thus equal to

$$(W^i + W^o) / 2W^i \qquad (12)$$

A unitary velocity emerges under our assumption that $W^i = W^o$.

4. Failure of the Plan and Partial Reform
(Decentralization without Price Liberalization)

Let us define partial reform as an attempt to decentralize some decisions, allowing more freedom to enterprises. One important aspect of this decentralization is that the choice of n is free. Moreover, firms can keep deposits in the bank. In addition, wages may be set with some degree of independence at the firm level.

If wages are set above the level consistent with equilibrium, there can be an excessive accumulation of money. Money overhang can be simply defined as the difference between the actual and the desired stocks of real monetary balances. This can be expressed in relation to output of consumption goods. Thus, money overhang can be defined as

$$\frac{M^h}{P^o y^o} - \frac{M^{*h}}{P^o y^o} \tag{13}$$

As noted by Sahay and Végh (1996), in this system a once-and-for-all increase in wages implies a permanent increase in money supply, which in a context of fixed output implies an ever-increasing monetary overhang.

It is apparent from the above model that the presence of a monetary overhang does not imply the presence of a *credit overhang*. This is possible because of the separation of household and enterprise monetary circuits. In fact, more generally, the credit system works as a pure trade credit system, with banks functioning as clearing houses. However, credit overhang could be defined as credit that financed accumulation of inventories above those required by the production plan.

4.1 Monetary Overhang and Inventories

Assuming wages and prices to be constant, let us focus on the case in which the plan does not work properly. Two cases can be distinguished. First, demand for consumption goods may exceed supply, thus giving rise to shortages. This is the case of monetary overhang alluded to above. Second, there can be investment hunger at the enterprise level. Abstracting from fixed investments, consumer-good firms purchase an amount of inputs in excess of their production needs. Inventories of inputs tend to grow continuously.

43

In the first case, the central bank finances wages in excess of the level required to balance demand and supply of consumer goods (see also Sahay and Végh 1996). In the second, the central bank finances the accumulation of inventories. The following extension of the model used in previous sections illustrates how excess inventories—and thus excess credit—may result in a monetary overhang in the household sector.

The accumulation of inventories is given by the difference between purchase of inputs and their use in production during period t:

$$S_t^i - S_{t-1}^i = y_t^i - n_t^i \qquad (14)$$

Let us assume, as in previous sections, that wages equal value added. However, accumulation of inventories is financed through interest-free revolving credit. Thus, in the consumer-good sector, wages are still equal to sales net of the value of inputs used in production. Thus total wages in the economy are

$$W_t^O + W_t^i = y_t^O - n_t^i + y_t^i > y_t^O \qquad (15)$$

Accumulation of money by households equals the difference between total wages and total consumption:

$$M_t^h - M_{t-1}^h = W_t^O + W_t^i - y_t^O = y_t^i - n_t^i = S_t^i - S_{t-1}^i \qquad (16)$$

Thus, the accumulation of input inventories results in an ever-growing stock of money in the household sector and in a monetary overhang. Can we define the perpetual credit as credit overhang? If we use the definition of monetary overhang as money that cannot be spent on goods, the above system does not generate a credit overhang. Indeed, the accumulated stock of inventories can repay the whole stock of credit accumulated over time. From this perspective, there is no credit overhang. From an efficiency point of view, the system is seriously flawed, as it directs a growing amount of resources to input-input activities and away from consumption.

If one adds a labor force constraint, which implies that the total labor employed in the two sectors is constrained by a constant labor force

$$L_t^o + L_t^i = N \qquad (17)$$

then it can be easily derived that the accumulation of input inventories, by drawing labor into the input sector, limits the supply of consumer goods. In a centrally planned economy, investment hunger derives from the objective of ensuring availability of inputs in a context of uncertain delivery and changing output targets of the planner. In partially reformed economies, inventories, together with foreign currency, represent one of the few available investment opportunities. Expectations of price reform thus induce firms to hoard goods. From this simple example it is also apparent that if wages in the consumer-good sector decline by the amount needed to finance inventory accumulation, there is no monetary overhang.

4.2 Effects of Price Liberalization

Let us assume, again for simplicity, that price liberalization leads to an increase in prices so that the monetary overhang can be ex ante eliminated (at unchanged real variables). Bank credit is kept constant in nominal terms; there is simply a rollover of old credit. Reforms change the nature of the constraints for the firms. Output-good firms now face a genuine cash-in-advance constraint. Assuming that input prices increase in the same proportion as output prices, the cash-in-advance constraint can be summarized by the following equation:

$$n_t^i \leq \frac{BC_t}{P_t^{i'}} \qquad (18)$$

Note that, as labor is a fixed factor, the input-good sector can produce the same level of output as in the prereform period. With the cash they obtain from the sale of inputs they can pay wages:

$$W_t^{i'} = P_t^{i'} n_t^{i'} \qquad (19)$$
$$n_t^{i'} = g(L_t^i)$$

As credit to output-good firms is unchanged in nominal terms, the nominal value of sales of inputs is unchanged as well. However, real wages in the input-good sector decline (both in terms of input and output good, which have the same price). Note also that real sales of input drop, while output remains unchanged. Thus, inventories in the input-good sector increase. Despite its over-simplification, the model accounts for three main facts (see Frydman and Wellisz 1991): the drop in real wages, the smaller fall in output in the input-good sectors relative to the consumption-good sectors, and the initial increase in inventories of finished products (or own-good inventories) (Berg and Blanchard 1994).

Let us now consider the output-good sector. Assuming that the consumption function is still a constant proportion of total labor income, the percentage change in sales is thus equal to the percentage change in total wages. Moreover, if we assume that the percentage change in wages is the same in the two sectors of the economy, it then follows that in the output-good sector the percentage change in sales is greater than the percentage change in output.

$$\frac{dy_t^s}{y_{t-1}} = \frac{dw_t}{w_t}$$

$$\frac{dy_t^o}{y_{t-1}} = \alpha \frac{dn_t}{n_{t-1}} \qquad (20)$$

$$\text{with } \alpha < 1$$

$$\frac{dw_t}{w_{t-1}} = \frac{dn_t}{n_{t-1}}$$

Thus, even in the last case, there is an initial accumulation of finished good inventories, taken by some observers as evidence of the importance of a demand shock rather than a credit contraction in determining the output decline (Berg and Blanchard 1994). In fact, the model shows that this phenomenon is consistent with a recession that is induced by a contraction of real credit to firms. The credit view of inventory behavior is in fact strengthened if one considers that most finished-good inventories are located in the trade sector, not in industry. If the trade sector operates on credit (both trade and bank credit), one obtains that following a credit contraction—and thus an increase in the cost of carrying inventories—the trade sector reduces its demand to industry, depleting its inventories. Thus, in order to ascertain exogenous changes in consumer demand, production in industry should be compared with industrial sales plus the decline of inventories in the trade sector (of course, changing its sign). Industrial production would be larger than industrial sales, as a result of the increase in inventories at the industry level. However, industrial production will be lower than the sum of industrial sales and the decline in inventories in the trade sector, a sum that proxies demand. As the bulk of finished-good inventories is held by the trade sector, the above result is likely to occur when one observes simultaneously an increase in inventories of finished goods in industry and a decline of finished-good inventories in the trade sector. Thus, what matters for aggregate demand is the change in the total stock of inventories, aggregating industry and trade sectors.

Evidence from Poland confirms the above argument. Table 2.1 clearly indicates that during 1989, in anticipation of full price liberalization, there was a sharp increase in inventories. The increase was particularly dramatic for input goods. This reinforced the typical structure of planned economies, in which—compared with market economies—ratios of inventories to sales are extremely high for input goods and very low for output or consumption goods.

Table 2.1

Poland: Inventories, End-of-Period Stocks over Annualized Sales

	1989.I	1989.IV	1990.I	1990.IV	1991.IV	1992.IV	1993.IV
Input	0,087	0,146	0,030	0,092	0,062	0,063	0,055
Unfinished products	0,029	0,040	0,009	0,039	0,036	0,042	0,038
Own output	0,010	0,015	0,004	0,023	0,028	0,030	0,030
Finished other	0,004	0,006	0,001	0,004	0,029	0,043	0,039
% change							
Input		67,92	-79,34	202,48	-32,24	1,61	-12,70
Unfinished products		39,81	-77,76	333,33	-7,69	16,67	-9,52
Own output		59,41	-76,39	538,89	21,74	7,14	-0,33
Finished other		49,66	-81,82	280,00	663,16	48,28	-10,23

Source: Polish Statistical Office (1994), Monthly Statistical Bulletin, Warsaw

With the introduction of full-fledged reforms in Poland in 1990, there was an initial downward adjustment in all categories of goods, followed by a recovery of finished-good inventories. Particularly significant is the sharp drop in input inventories, which signals the tightening of liquidity conditions for firms. The fall in finished-good inventories in the first quarter, when the collapse of production took place, seems to signal two main forces at work at the beginning of stabilization. The first is the credibility of the stabilization program. The massive drawdown of inventories suggests that firms expected inflation to stabilize and thus cashed the capital gains from the accumulation of inventories carried out during 1989. Second, liquidity constraints on firms were biting, and firms tried to soften the liquidity crunch by using their inventories.[2] It is remarkable that the ratio of input inventories to sales increased after the first quarter of 1990. In fact, following the relaxation of credit policy during the second half of 1990, the ratio increased significantly above the average level that characterized the following years. A similar pattern is observed for finished-good inventories. If one adds the behavior of inventories in the trade sector, a clear picture emerges of a sharp contraction of finished-good inventories at the outset of the Polish stabilization. For the first quarter of 1990, statistical analysis confirms the importance of credit in explaining inventory behavior at the outset of stabilization. Table 2.2 shows the statistically significant positive effect of credit on inventories.

Table 2.2

Poland: Regressions on Inventories and Credit, 1990.I/1989.IV

Dependent variable: change in input inventories
Two stage least squares
Observations: 85

Variable	Coefficient	t-statistics
Constant	0.36	5.78
Change in credit	0.18	2.40
Change in sales	0.33	4.44

Instruments: constant; change in sales and ratio of bank credit to material costs in 1989.IV.

4.2.1 The Role of Initial Inventories

Let us consider the case in which there is a stock of excessive inventories at the outset of reforms. If postreform prices were perfectly flexible and determined by demand and supply forces, one would have observed an increase in consumer prices to eliminate the monetary overhang, and a *decline* in the price of inputs, driven by the depletion of inventories. However, inputs are generally tradable goods, and their initial level was well below world prices. As stabilization started with large devaluations, the price of inputs jumped at the beginning of reforms. Moreover, the price of raw materials continued to be controlled after reforms. Thus, the increase in the price of some key input was determined by policy decision. The price of inputs increased sharply, even more than the price of consumer goods. If credit had been used only to accumulate excessive inventories, the outcome of the combination of increasing input prices and constant nominal credit would have been the following: as the flow of credit stopped, inventory accumulation would stop as well. The old stock of inventories would increase in value (in terms of consumer goods). The balance sheet of firms would significantly improve, the nominal debt remaining unchanged, while the value of real assets (inventories) increased. If realized—by using inventories, or by selling them abroad—the capital gain would be partly taxed, and the rest absorbed by higher profits. The country as a whole would experience a current account surplus, or a simultaneous increase in exports and imports, if the capital gain were passed on to the consumers (through higher wages, for instance).

This optimistic scenario is far from the actual experience of PCPEs. One main reason is that credit was not simply financing excess inventories, but normal working capital as well. Thus, the sharp increase in input prices implied the need for higher credit. Inventory depletion could only partially compensate the fall in real credit. Moreover, the drop in inventories implied the decline in demand for the output of input-producing firms.[3] Thus, even with inventories, the risk of a credit crunch cannot be ruled out. Note that maintaining the old stock of real credit would imply an accommodation of the initial price-level jump, with no further implications for inflation.

So far we have illustrated some of the main effects ensuing from an initial credit crunch. Let us now discuss in a two-period setting the effects under different assumptions on credit markets. Three cases will be compared: a bank credit equilibrium; a pure trade credit equilibrium; and, finally, a money or cash equilibrium.

4.3 Bank Credit Equilibrium

As shown in the preceding section, input-good firms act passively. We can thus focus on the output-good firms. These firms maximize the discounted value of the stream of labor income over the life of the firm (two periods). Thus

$$\max \ w_t^o + \frac{w_{t+1}^o}{1+r} \tag{21}$$

where r is the subjective rate of time preference—assumed for simplicity's sake to be equal to the world interest rate—subject to the constraints

$$y_t - n_t - w_t^o - (1+i)bc_{t-1} = m_{t+1} - m_t$$

$$y_{t+1} - n_{t+1} - w_{t+1}^o - (1+i)bc_t = m_{t+2} - m_{t+1} \tag{22}$$

$$n_t = m_t + bc_t$$

$$n_{t+1} = m_{t+1}$$

$$y_t = f(n_t) \quad \forall t$$

$$m_{t+2} = 0$$

Let us define $f(.)$ as a net output function $(y - n)$. Using the first two constraints to solve for w in the two periods, and using the cash-in-advance constraints, we can substitute into the objective function to obtain:

$$U = f(\overline{m} + bc_t) - m_{t+1} - (1+i)bc_{t-1} + \frac{f(m_{t+1}) - (1+i)bc_t}{1+r} \tag{23}$$

The first-order conditions for this problem are obtained by differentiating the objective function with respect to b_{ct} and m_{t+1}.

$$f'(\overline{m} + bc_t) = \frac{1+i}{1+r}$$

$$f'(m_{t+1}) = 1+r \qquad (24)$$

Note that imperfections in credit markets can be summarized by the difference between i and r. In particular, $i > r$ summarizes inefficient domestic credit markets, assuming r equal to the world real interest rate. Short-term output is a decreasing function of the rate of interest; real wages in period two decline as well with the rate of interest. If the government sets ceilings on bank credit, the solution is trivial. Output in period one is predetermined, while the optimal solution applies in the second period. As in the previous section, if the ceiling implies a reduction in real credit, output declines on impact. When the government uses the interest rate as instrument, the above solution applies.

4.4 Trade Credit Equilibrium

Under our assumption that wages are paid at the end of the period, a trade credit equilibrium can replicate the prereform level of real output and real wages. Trade credit permits the purchase of inputs and, in the aggregate, permits firms to avoid accumulating monetary inventories. As a result, as long as relative prices do not change, real equilibrium does not change as well.

A simple corollary of the result shown above is that the larger the trade credit is at the outset of reform, the lower the contraction in output is likely to be. Under pure trade credit, firms maximize their objective function subject to the intertemporal budget constraint, and there is no leakage of resources to the banking system. The relevant time discount rate is equal to the world interest rate, and thus

$$\max \quad w_t^o + \frac{w_{t+1}^o}{1+r}$$

$$s.to \tag{25}$$

$$f(n_t) - n_t + \frac{f(n_{t+1})}{1+r} -$$

The first-order conditions for an optimum are

$$f'(n_t) = 1$$

$$f'(n_{t+1}) = 1 + r \tag{26}$$

The first conditions simply states that firms will try to purchase the maximum amount of inputs available. Assuming that the production of inputs is finite, given the finite amount of labor in the input-good sector, it follows that

$$n_t = n_{max} \tag{27}$$

Thus, first-period output is maximized under the trade credit equilibrium (see Townsend 1990 for a general model and historical discussion of trade credit).

4.4.1 Correlation between Bank Credit and Trade Credit

Note that in this setting the issue of the correlation between trade credit and bank credit can also be addressed. For small changes in the cost or quantity of bank credit, the correlation between bank credit and trade credit tends to be negative, as firms substitute the two forms of credit. Indeed, there is no major change in the perceived risk of default on trade credit. In contrast, a large contraction of bank credit—or an increase in its cost—sharply increases the probability of finding insolvent firms down the chain of inter-enterprise transactions. Thus, trade credit could contract as well. In Poland, at the outset of stabilization the correlation between the two forms of credit was positive.

4.5 Money-Only Equilibrium

Money-only equilibrium is analogous to the equilibrium studied in Calvo and Coricelli (1992). The cash-in-advance constraints are simply

$$n_t = m_t = \overline{m}$$
$$n_{t+1} = m_{t+1}$$

(28)

while the accumulation of real monetary balances takes the following form:

$$f(m_t) - w_t^o = m_{t+1}$$

(29)

If firms maximize the same objective function as in the previous section, the first-order condition is simply

$$f'(m_{t+1}) = 1 + r$$

(30)

The above condition determines optimal output in period two. Output in period one is predetermined and equal to $f(m_t)$, with m given by history. If initial m is below its optimal level given by the first order condition (equation 30), wages in the first period will fall below their level in the second period, and this will allow the firm to accumulate the optimal level of m. Note that the maximum gap between the bank credit and the money-only equilibrium arises when $i=r$, thus when the banking sector is efficient. Thus, the money-only solution becomes attractive when there are larger imperfections in the financial sector. In the money-only equilibrium, output in the first period can be below its optimal long-run level because of the cash-in-advance constraint. The latter is avoided only in the trade credit equilibrium.

The gap between the bank credit and the money-only equilibria depends as well on the initial level of monetary holdings. For very low initial levels of real monetary balances in firms, the bank credit equilibrium tends to lead to higher total output than the money-only equilibrium, even when the inefficiency in the banking system is large; thus, the premium of i over r is high. In economies beginning reforms from a highly centralized system in which monetary holdings by enterprises were generally forbidden, reliance on self-financing tends to lead to a sharp initial fall in output, although long-run output converges to output achieved using bank credit.

4.6 Interenterprise Arrears: Equilibria with Default

If one allows for the possibility of default on payments to other enterprises (interenterprise arrears), a different liquidity constraint for firms arises. Arrears are a form of involuntary trade credit. In the model with money one can see that the return to arrears is given by the real interest rate—the rate at which workers can invest their funds. However, differently from voluntary trade credit, arrears are likely to generate costs. Assuming that these costs take the form of a loss of output for the "offender," one can obtain multiple equilibria (Calvo and Coricelli 1994). In particular, there is an equilibrium with zero default, identical to the money-only equilibrium discussed above. In addition, there is an equilibrium with maximum default: firms pay the minimum amount, probably what is necessary to pay for wages (see Calvo and Coricelli 1994 for evidence for the case of Romania).

Let us assume only a share θ of sales will be paid. Given that the international price of inputs and outputs is equal to 1, the price set by firms on domestic transactions will be $1/\theta$. Defaulting on payment has a cost for the offender. As in Calvo and Coricelli (1994), we assume that the marginal cost is an exogenous parameter, κ. Thus, total cost is proportional to the arrears. One can conjecture that these costs vary across countries, and probably across sectors in the same country. Moreover, the penalty may be a function of the different nature of the loans: thus, perceived penalties on arrears of different forms (with other enterprises, government, and banks) are likely to be different. This implies different degrees of default across different debts. As shown below, this seems to be borne out by data on Poland.

As stated in Calvo and Coricelli (1994), a more realistic setting would make such cost of default a decreasing function of the total amount of arrears in the economy. One way to extend the model in this direction is to assume that in cases of default, firms must liquidate assets used as collateral. The liquidation value of these assets is likely to be a function of the total amount of assets liquidated. In terms of the model, this implies that the individual cost of default depends on aggregate arrears. This may explain how a generalized default can come about. With heterogeneous firms, the model can rationalize the fact that even firms that are able to pay will not, if the return of falling into arrears is larger than the cost. One can think in terms of a long chain in which some firms are liquidity constrained. When liquidity unexpectedly falls, they cannot pay. This implies that suppliers of these firms will suffer a revenue shortfall. It may happen that such shortfall is not large enough to put them in a situation of inevitable default. Depending on the number of firms that have defaulted, the non-liquidity-constrained firms can break or continue the chain, depending on the cost of default. This may explain the evidence that shows the presence of countries in which the chain of default is interrupted, and thus default is a local phenomenon, and of other countries where there is generalized default.[4]

Let x denote non-labor inputs purchased by the firm. Given the above assumptions, liquidity of firms evolves according to the following expression when the firm falls into arrears:

$$M_{t+1} = f(x_t) - \kappa \left(\frac{x_t}{\theta_t} - M_t \right) - \omega_t \qquad (31)$$

Workers still maximize the present value of the stream of their wages over the life of the firm. Calvo and Coricelli (1994) show that the model produces multiple equilibria. There is a continuum of interior equilibria that emerge when the marginal cost of arrears κ equals the marginal return on arrears, that is the interest rate r workers can get by investing the money saved from not paying for inputs. In addition to these interior equilibria, there are two more relevant corner equilibria. One is in which the return on arrears is greater than the cost and thus arrears reach their maximum level. The other occurs when the cost is greater than the benefit and thus arrears do not take place, and firms pay with money for their purchases of inputs. The latter equilibrium is identical to the money-only equilibrium analyzed above. The two types of equilibria can be ranked in terms of aggregate output in the economy, with the one with maximum arrears displaying the lowest level of output.

4.6.1 Money as an Externality and Interenterprise Arrears

In the analysis of arrears, the condition determining different types of equilibria linked the value of the cost of arrears (the marginal cost of arrears) to the return of arrears. The higher inflation is, the higher the return to default becomes, while the cost remains unchanged. Thus, not only may arrears lead to higher inflation by forcing the government to loosen monetary policy, but inflation itself fosters arrears. It is now possible for a vicious circle to be activated.

This phenomenon suggests a more general view of money in the context of the high costs of enforcing credit contracts. If most firms use money, the individual firm will also carry monetary holdings and use money for interenterprise payments. Thus, there is an externality in the demand for money. The higher the monetary holdings of other firms, the higher will be the demand for money of the firm. The average stock of money holdings thus enters as an argument of the demand for money function of the single firm. In turn, the aggregate stock of money exerts a positive effect on output (Farmer 1993).

This view has interesting implications for the analysis of money demand and the effects of monetary policy on inflation, especially when monetary authorities try to solve the payment crisis through injection of new money into the system. One possible chain of events is as follows. At the start of reforms credit is sharply cut. Interenterprise arrears explode. The central bank reacts to this by issuing credit to enterprises. This increase in credit, in principle, may not be inflationary as it substitutes bank credit for interenterprise credit. However, such substitution may end up being partial, as individual firms will reduce their degree of default on new payments to other firms only if they believe all other firms will do the same. Therefore, there is scope for multiple self-fulfilling equilibria. If firms assume other firms will continue defaulting on their payments, they will follow suit. As a result, demand for money will not increase, and the newly-injected money will fuel inflation. For instance, in the case of Ukraine, the aggregate that seems to matter for economic activity, and the aggregate that responds in a predictable way to changes in inflation, is the sum of money and arrears, rather than money alone (as shown in section 6).

5. Loanable Funds and Money Demand

So far we have focused on a situation in which bank credit is not constrained by the funds available to banks. However, in actual economies, bank lending is constrained by the availability of funds (loanable funds), which in turn depends on deposits that economic actors, especially households, are willing to keep in the banks. Calvo and Kumar (1994) discuss this issue in the context of a simple model similar to ours. From a theoretical point of view, there is not any essential insight gained from considering explicitly the relationship between money demand and credit. Indeed, in models with money in the production function, inflation reduces the level of output. In the model with money demand by households, inflation reduces money demand, and thus loanable funds, which in turn reduce liquidity of enterprises and their ability to buy inputs. The end result is a decline in production. Nevertheless, explicit consideration of money demand helps in illustrating the working of various channels. We therefore incorporate money demand in our model (following Calvo and Kumar 1994).

A simple result is that inflation has generally adverse effects on output. However, depending on the sources of money creation, there can be a trade-off between inflation and output. This is the case in which money creation has a direct effect on the cash-in-advance constraint of enterprises, as for instance with money-financed subsidies to enterprises, or tax arrears financed by money creation. Similarly, if the state owns banks, default on payments to banks may loosen the liquidity constraint for enterprises and, at the same time, create a budgetary problem through a loss of income by the state bank.

If we define H as base money, M as broad money and B as bank credit, then

$$B_t + H_t = M_t \tag{32}$$

Let us define v as the compulsory reserve requirements on bank deposits. Thus, broad money can be expressed as

$$H_t = v \ M_t \tag{33}$$

Using the above identities, bank credit can be expressed as

$$\frac{B_t}{P_t} = (1-v) \ \frac{M_t}{P_t} \tag{34}$$

If we assume money demand is a function of inflation, and that there is equilibrium in the money market, then

$$\frac{B_t}{P_t} = (1-v) \ \frac{M^d(\pi_{t+1})}{P_t} \tag{35}$$

Focusing, for simplicity, on a case in which bank credit is the only source of liquidity for firms, the liquidity constraint can be defined as

$$n_t = \frac{B_t}{P_t} = (1-v) \ \frac{M^d(\pi_{t+1})}{P_t} \tag{36}$$

The above equation highlights the relationship between money demand and output. Higher inflation reduces output through its negative effect on money demand and thus loanable funds. Moreover, for a given money demand, higher reserve requirements reduce output. More generally, the parameter of reserve requirement can be interpreted as a proxy of the share of loan supply in total bank assets. For instance, an increase in the holding of securities by banks reduces loan supply as well—although by less than reserve requirements, as banks earn higher interest on securities than on reserves.

As shown by Calvo and Kumar (1994), if money creation results from subsidies to enterprises, the liquidity constraint for the latter becomes

$$\frac{B_t}{P_t} + \frac{H_{t+1} - H_t}{P_t} = n_t \tag{37}$$

Substituting for H and B, one obtains

$$n_t = (1 - v + v \pi_{t+1}) M_t^d(\pi_{t+1}) \tag{38}$$

From the above expression one can derive a trade-off between inflation and output. The positive term in brackets indicates the positive direct effect of inflation (subsidies) on output. However, there is also the indirect effect of the reduction in money demand induced by higher inflation. Depending on the value of the reserve requirement ratio and of the elasticity of money demand with respect to inflation, the effect of inflation on output can be positive or negative. Also, as the negative effect is multiplied by the inflation rate, it turns out that the higher the inflation rate, the more likely that the effect will be negative.

A simple estimation of money demand in Poland after reforms helps to give a quantitative assessment of the potential trade-off. Results of regressions are reported in table 2.3. Using the reserve requirement ratio for 1993 (23 percent on demand and savings deposits) and a monthly inflation of 2 percent, the estimated coefficient in the money demand for total *M2* implies that

$$\frac{d\,n_{\,t}}{d\,\pi_{\,t+1}} \tag{39}$$

is positive in the short run, but negative in the long run. The output gain from an inflationary financed subsidy is thus short-lived.

Table 2.3

Poland: Money Demand and Inflation, 1990.1–1994.10

OLS regression, Observations: 58
Dependent variable: log of real M2

Variable	t-statistics	Coefficient
Constant	-0.26	-1.66
Refinancing interest rate	0.01	3.79
Inflation rate	-1.48	-9.21
Log of real M2 (-1)	0.98	16.27
Log of industrial production	0.07	1.99
Adjusted R-squared	0.85	
Durbin-Watson	1.65	

As discussed below, the rough estimates obtained indicate that the inflation tax may be quite harmful in a country such as Poland. However, as shown in the model, the losses from the inflation tax may be compensated by improvements in the efficiency of the banking system (lower ν). Recent policies in Poland seem to be partly misplaced. Indeed, the apparent conservative policy on recapitalization of banks has led to an increase in tax arrears. Moreover, incentives for commercial banks have been made to increase safe assets rather than the effective supply of loans. A more efficient banking system should imply a lower, not a higher ν, as discussed below.

5.1 Inflation, Liquidity Constraints, and Growth

The model can offer an explanation for the observed stagflationary feature of the initial stages of transition. Let us assume that in the model of default in section 4.6, we consider the possibility of inflation (Calvo and Coricelli 1994). Inflation increases the return on arrears. As there are two regions separated by a threshold level of inflation, the model predicts that to generate the socially inferior equilibrium—with generalized default—inflation has to be sufficiently large. Until inflation reaches that level, it has no effect on the equilibrium. In fact, if inflation reflects subsidies to firms, it may even imply a higher output. This may contribute to an explanation for why even successful countries were characterized by relatively high rates of inflation.

It is well known that when money serves a productive role— and thus is like a factor of production—inflation has a negative effect on output. With inflation, the first-order condition for an optimum in the model of section 4.5 becomes, in steady state,

$$f'(m) = (1+r)(1+\pi) = (1+i) \tag{40}$$

where π is the rate of inflation, and i the nominal interest rate. Thus, the higher inflation is, the lower the stock of real money and thus the lower the level of output. The nonlinearity between inflation and output—namely the fact that high inflation seems highly detrimental to growth, but low inflation has no clear impact on growth—may arise when the relationship between inflation and money demand is taken into account. When inflation is driven by monetary financing of subsidies to firms, two different Laffer curves are obtained (Calvo and Kumar 1994). One is the standard bell-shaped relationship between inflation and revenues from the inflation tax. The other is a bell-shaped relationship between inflation and output. After the maximum is reached, increasing inflation leads to lower output. The intuition is that inflation sustains output as it finances subsidies that directly stimulate output. However, by reducing money demand, inflation reduces loanable funds, credit to firms, and thus output. The higher the level of inflation, the more likely that the second, negative effect dominates the positive effect on output.

Other nonlinearities have been identified. For instance, De Gregorio and Sturzenegger (1994) show an example in which there is a threshold of inflation. Past the threshold the allocation of credit becomes inefficient, reducing the rate of growth of the economy. Perhaps one fundamental source of nonlinearity in the case of economies in transition is the role of inflation in pushing the economy toward a bad equilibrium in a context of multiple equilibria, as in the case of interenterprise arrears.

6. Empirical Evidence (Hungary, Poland, Romania, Russia, and Ukraine)

As noted earlier, all stabilization programs, except for Hungary in 1990 and the former Yugoslavia in 1990, implied a sharp fall in real money and credit aggregates. Velocity of circulation increased sharply in several countries. It is worth noting that in Hungary, the Czech Republic, and Slovakia, velocity steadily declined during the

Table 2.4

Panel Regression: Velocity of Circulation of Broad Money, 1989–94*

	Coefficients	t-statistics
Constant	2.16	8.55
Rate of inflation	0.004	3.96
R2	0.21	
Sample:	54 observations	

*Countries: Bulgaria, Czech Republic, Estonia, Hungary, Latvia, Lithuania, Poland, Romania, Slovakia

Figure 2.1

**Russia: Velocity of Money and Arrears, 1992.02–1995.06
(Inflation Right Scale)**

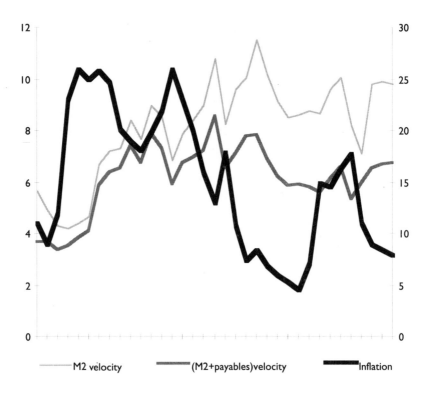

───── M2 velocity   ━━━━━ (M2+payables)velocity   ▬▬▬ Inflation

Source: Russian Economic Trends (1995), Moscow

reform period. In countries where inflation was brought under
control, velocity declined after the initial blip. In countries such as
Romania, Russia, and Ukraine, velocity continued to increase after
the initial adjustment. A panel regression on nine countries of
Central and Eastern Europe and the Baltics during the period
1989-94 shows the sensitivity of the behavior of velocity with
respect to the rate of inflation (table 2.4).

Figure 2.1a

Ukraine: Velocity and Arrears, 1993.01–1995.06

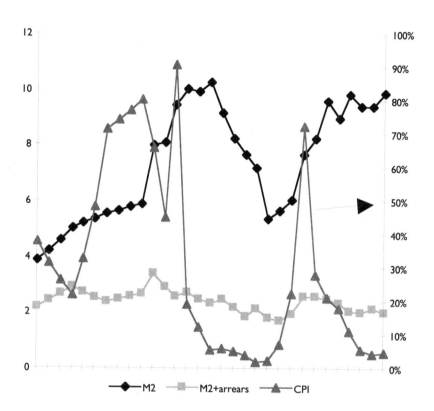

Source: Ukrainian Economic Trends (1995), Kiev

In contrast, the relationship between velocity and inflation appears weak and unstable in countries such as Russia and Ukraine (figures 2.1 and 2.1a). In both countries, the decline in the rate of inflation was not accompanied by a decline in velocity. For these countries, we argue that a major determinant of money velocity was the behavior of interenterprise arrears. Note that in Ukraine, for instance, bank credit was a minor component of credit in the system. Interenterprise arrears were ten to fifteen times larger than bank credit. In such a context, a monetary/credit policy that neglects arrears is not very meaningful.

Overall, some of the main facts seem to be consistent with the model outlined in previous sections. The model implies an increase in velocity—a fall in credit/money to output ratios—if the elasticity of output with respect to credit/money aggregates is smaller than one. Estimates for Poland (Calvo and Coricelli 1993) indicate an elasticity of about 20 percent. Moreover, three additional forces may have contributed to the increase in velocity. First, in countries with monetary overhang there would be an initial increase in velocity, as money demand drops to its equilibrium level. Second, if firms were holding excessive input inventories, they would reduce the credit-to-output ratio by depleting their stocks of inventories. Finally, a key role is played by the substitutability between bank credit aggregates and private credit, mainly trade credit or interenterprise arrears.

The importance of credit markets goes beyond the initial phases of stabilization. In fact, several observers emphasize the central role of credit markets in affecting the long-term growth of transition economies (EBRD Transition Report 1995; Cornelli et al. 1996). In this respect, both the magnitude and—perhaps even more important—the allocation of credit play a key role. In the next sections we review some empirical evidence on the functioning of credit markets in economies in transition. First, we analyze the role played by the banking system in countries where reforms were successful, at least from a macroeconomic point of view. In particular, we explore whether banks supported the adjustment and the recovery of the economy.

We then turn to an analysis of the role of the financial sector in determining different adjustment paths after stabilization. The focus is on the development of credit markets and the possibility of development of dysfunctional market institutions as a response to a monetary squeeze. We argue that the blossoming of interenterprise arrears is an example of such dysfunctional private markets and contrast the experience of countries where arrears grew into a systemic problem (Romania, Russia, and Ukraine) with countries in which a well-functioning voluntary trade market developed (Hungary and Poland).

6.1 Financing the Recovery in More Advanced Reformers: Bank Credit and Trade Credit During Transition, the Case of Poland and Hungary

As shown in earlier sections, after three years from the start of reforms, economies tended to recover from the initial deep recession. Credit seems to have played an important role in the initial output collapse. Even less controversial is the fact that a *credit crunch* characterized most economies in the second stage of reforms. Financial discipline seems to have been imposed especially in Central and Eastern European countries. Under severe credit constraints, and lacking subsidies, firms operated under pressure to minimize their costs. While in several cases such hardening of liquidity constraints may produce a positive adjustment by firms, the role of the financial sector should be that of fostering growth by channeling resources to the most efficient users. Evidence provided in several studies (King and Levine 1993, among others) indicates a fundamental relationship between the level of financial intermediation and growth. Thus, the low level of financial intermediation in PCPEs raises concern about the sustainability of growth. In this regard, after five to six years since the

Table 2.5

Poland: Interest Rate Spreads

	1989	1990	1991	1992	1993	1994
Prime lending rate	169.0	61.0	49.0	49.5	45.0	40.2
Short-term deposit rate	115.0	43.5	35.5	33.5	25.5	25.0
Spread						
in percentage points	54.0	17.5	13.5	16.0	19.5	15.2
in percent	47.0	40.2	38.0	47.8	76.5	60.8
memo items:*						
CPI		77.0	45.0	46.0	42.0	27.0
PPI		55.0	24.0	28.0	34.0	20.0
Real lending rate		3.9	20.2	16.8	8.2	16.8
Real deposit rate		-18.9	-6.6	-8.6	-11.6	-1.6

* Inflation is calculated as the annualized rate for the last quarter of the year.

Source: Polish Statistical Office (1995), Monthly Statistical Bulletin, Warsaw

start of reforms, financial systems appear highly inefficient, even in the most advanced reformers. Real interest rates grew to levels that discourage borrowing by viable firms. Moreover, spreads between lending and borrowing rates remained high. The presence of bad loans in the portfolio of banks only partially explains such phenomenon. For instance, in Poland the interest rate spreads remained very high, both in percentage points and in percent even after the recapitalization of banks under the plan for dealing with bad loans (table 2.5).

In Hungary and Poland, where the financing of budget deficits increasingly relied on government bonds, banks have reduced the share of loans in favor of safer government bonds in their assets. Although the persistence of relatively high rates of inflation and the uncertainty associated with large-scale structural change in the economy may justify the reluctance of banks to extend long-term loans, the crunch on short-term credit reveals the inefficiency of the banking system.

The next sections attempt to analyze in more detail the possible inefficiencies in the allocation of credit, focusing on microeconomic data on Hungary and Poland.

6.2 The Allocation of Credit: An Analysis of Microeconomic Data

This section uses microeconomic data on borrowing firms to analyze the characteristics of financial markets in order to assess the main factors driving the allocation of credit among firms. Due to data availability the analysis covers two countries, Hungary and Poland. These countries belong to the group of advanced reformers. The objective of the analysis is to identify the factors affecting the distribution of credit across firms.

Regarding bank credit, three main aspects were considered. The first consideration is the relationship between profitability of firms and credit allocation. In general, the sign of such relationship is ambiguous because the reduced form estimation summarizes a demand effect and a supply effect. The demand effect may be negative, as more profitable, possibly more liquid firms demand less credit and rely more on self-financing. The supply effect, describing the behavior of banks, should be positive, if profits reflected the underlying viability of firms. Second, we investigate the importance of collateral in the allocation of credit. We tried several measures of collateral, such as the ratio of fixed capital to total assets and financial assets over financial liabilities. Third, we

Table 2.6

Poland: Degree of Concentration of Bank Credit, 1993

Largest firms ranked by bank credit, shares in total

Number of firms	Sales	Bank credit
(a) State sector		
20	0.58	0.58
30	0.62	0.46
50	0.70	0.52
70	0.76	0.60
100	0.84	0.72
(b) Private sector		
20	0.13	0.53
30	0.19	0.60
50	0.24	0.68
70	0.30	0.74
100	0.38	0.80

Source: Polish Statistical Office, 3-digit dataset provided to the author

explore the possible presence of asymmetries in the treatment of firms in different ownership categories. The analysis then extends to the role of trade credit and its relationship with bank credit. Finally, for the case of Poland we examine the financing of loss-making firms and the different degrees of default on payments towards banks, enterprises, and the government.

6.2.1 Low Leverage and a High Degree of Concentration of Bank Credit

The aggregate picture hides significant heterogeneity within the state and, especially, the private sector aggregates. In Poland it is particularly important that bank credit is highly concentrated within the private sector. This implies that a large proportion of private firms are "credit free." By contrast, in the state sector bank credit is more evenly distributed (table 2.6). A similar phenomenon is observed in Hungary; however, in Hungary bank credit is relatively concentrated even in the state sector.[5]

The low levels of leverage and of credit-to-output ratios observed in Hungary and Poland reflect the high degree of concentration of debt in a small number of firms. This phenomenon is partly a function of firm size. Small- and medium-sized firms, gen-

Table 2.7

Regressions on Bank Credit, Microeconomic Data: Poland, 1992–94

3-digit industries
Tobit estimation

Dependent variable: Ratio of bank credit to sales

	1992		1993		1994	
	Coeff.	t-stat.	Coeff.	t-stat.	Coeff.	t-stat.
Constant	-0.14	-0.59	0.13	6.21	0.16	5.19
Profit/sales	-0.18	-0.65	-0.75	-3.55	0.17	1.33
Losses/sales	1.18	19.69	0.31	6.69	1.41	13.62
Ownership dummy*	.05	1.91	-0.03	-1.45	-0.08	-2.69

Observations: 1135 for 1992; 1196 for 1993; 1140 for 1994

* Ownership dummy: 1 = private firms; 0 = state firms

erally private, tend to be cut off from bank loans. By contrast, an opposite pattern characterizes some market economies, whereby small- and medium-sized firms are more bank credit dependent than large firms. In Italy, for instance, where small- and medium-sized firms account for a rather large proportion of industrial activity, the ratio of short-term bank credit to sales is a decreasing function of size.[6]

6.2.2 Characteristics and Determinants of Bank Credit and Trade Credit

We ran cross-section regressions for the years 1992–94 to analyze the determinants of the allocation of bank credit and of trade credit across branches.

6.2.2.1 Bank Credit

Poland. We isolated two main issues: first, the relationship between financial conditions of firms, summarized by profitability and bank credit; second, the relationship between ownership and bank credit. Regarding the role of profitability, the results indicate a highly inefficient distribution of credit, and its persistence over time. Indeed, firms displaying high losses in relation to sales are likely to obtain high bank credit in relation to sales.[7] The regressions indicate that allocation of credit remains skewed toward loss-making firms, which in 1994 still absorbed more than 50 percent of bank credit (table 2.7).

Regarding the ownership variable, results are ambiguous. Only in 1994 is there a statistically significant negative relationship between bank credit and a dummy for ownership. The negative sign indicates that in the whole sample the distribution of credit is skewed toward state firms. Ownership clearly matters, even after controlling for profitability.[8] Collateral does not appear as a relevant variable in the allocation of credit. Lacking a direct measure of physical capital, we estimated the stock of capital from data on depreciation. The proxy used does not lead to statistically significant results.

Table 2.8

Hungary: Bank Credit 1989–93

(a)   State firms

Dependent variable: Bank Credit as a Share of Sales

Variable	1989		1990		1991		1992		1993	
	Coeff.	t-stat.	Coeff.	t-stat.	Coeff.	t-stat.	Coeff.	t-stat.	Coeff.	t-stat.
Constant	0.04	13.25	0.05	12.30	0.03	8.10	0.02	0.43	0.14	5.41
Profit/sales	0.03	1.71	-0.13	-8.52	-0.16	-13.33	-0.15	-14.59	-0.38	-8.12
Collateral*	-0.03	-3.58	0.04	2.95	0.12	8.86	0.20	14.73	-0.05	-1.20

* Fixed assets/Total assets

(b)   Private firms

Dependent variable: Bank Credit as a Share of Sales

Variable	1989		1990		1991		1992		1993	
	Coeff.	t-stat.	Coeff.	t-stat.	Coeff.	t-stat.	Coeff.	t-stat.	Coeff.	t-stat.
Constant	0.02	6.65	0.03	10.83	0.02	9.40	0.00	3.00	0.07	4.03
Profit/sales	0.08	7.77	-0.07	-14.46	-0.12	-27.15	-0.05	-18.01	-0.10	-5.59
Collateral *	0.01	1.12	0.16	13.27	0.02	18.95	0.21	34.78	0.12	2.93

* Fixed assets/Total assets

Hungary. The analysis of the allocation of bank credit in Hungary broadly confirms the findings obtained for Poland.[9] We carried out a regression analysis for the period 1989-93 on enterprise data (table 2.8). The robust result in the regressions is that profitability is negatively related to bank credit. Interestingly, this holds for every ownership category, which suggests that it is the high cost of credit that deters profitable firms from borrowing. There seems to be a phenomenon of adverse selection.[10]

As found by Cornelli et al. (1996), collateral—measured as the ratio of fixed assets to total assets—is negatively correlated with leverage. This holds for regressions both on stocks and on flows. Moreover, Cornelli et al. (1996) found that the role of collateral differs for short-term and long-term credit. For the latter, the sign of collateral is positive. However, as long-term debt generally finances fixed investments, the positive correlation between the two is natural and does not reflect any behavioral rule followed by banks. If one analyzes flows of credit, then the ratio of fixed to total assets can be interpreted as collateral. When looking at flows, Cornelli et al. (1996) found that the collateral is statistically insignificant.

Given the possible unreliability of the measure of assets and the possible heterogeneity of different components of debt, we ran regressions on credit as a ratio of sales. Using such indicator as a dependent variable, we found that collateral has the expected positive sign and the coefficient is statistically significant most of the time for both state and private firms. The results indicate that collateral plays a crucial role in the allocation of credit. This reflects a form of market behavior on the part of the banks and indicates that they tend to be very cautious in lending. Nevertheless, this does not imply that credit is allocated to the more efficient firms. In fact, the profit indicator reveals that the opposite is true. Furthermore, as many new firms suffer from lack of collateral, the conservative behavior of the banks is likely to cut the most dynamic firms off the credit market.[11] Note that most firms are excluded from short-term financing. This implies that the enterprise sector as a whole, *unless it finances interenterprise transactions with trade credit,* has to hold monetary inventories that could instead be financing investment. As shown in section 4.5, the money-only equilibrium tends to lead to lower output than the equilibrium with bank credit.

Table 2.9

Poland: Degree of Concentration of Trade Credit, 1993

Largest firms ranked by trade credit (payables)

Number of firms	Sales	Trade credit
(a) State sector		
20	0.64	0.76
30	0.70	0.81
50	0.77	0.87
70	0.81	0.91
100	0.86	0.94
(b) Private sector		
20	0.17	0.26
30	0.23	0.33
50	0.30	0.42
70	0.38	0.50
100	0.48	0.59

Source: Polish Statistical Office, 3-digit dataset provided to the author

Thus, despite progress in financial sector reform, even in the most advanced countries the banking sector continues to allocate credit inefficiently. Growing firms, especially new private firms, tend to be almost "bank credit free." This phenomenon is partly natural, given the lack of information on new firms, the lack of collateral, and the high risk associated with innovations characterizing the activities of new firms. However, it is remarkable that many firms do not use bank loans to finance working capital. This puts pressure on firms for holding large cash balances or finding alternative sources of financing, such as trade credit or foreign loans. Indeed, it appears that a key role in supporting growing firms in Hungary was played by trade credit markets; this was also especially true in the case of Poland, while in the Czech Republic foreign loans played an important role, allowing firms to bypass the inefficiency of the domestic banking sector.

6.2.2.2 Trade Credit

Similarly to market economies, trade credit in Hungary and Poland represents a fundamental source of financing interenterprise transactions. In Poland, trade credit—measured by payables—of industrial firms in 1994 was 30 percent larger than short-term

Table 2.10

Poland: Trade Credit, Payables

(a) All industrial firms

Poland: 3-digit industries;
Tobit estimation
Observations: 1135 for 1992; 1196 for 1993; 1140 for 1994

	1992		1993		1994	
	Coeff.	t-stat.	Coeff.	t-stat.	Coeff.	t-stat.
Constant	-0.01	-0.73	0.07	8.60	-0.04	-2.34
Profit/sales	-0.22	-1.05	-0.36	-2.84	0.22	2.22
Losses/sales	0.41	7.72	0.29	9.46	1.89	20.80
Credit/sales	-0.11	-4.59	0.03	1.37	0.04	1.58
Receivables/sales	1.18	14.55	0.46	10.31	0.72	13.75

(b) Private firms

Poland: 3-digit industries;
Tobit estimation
Observations: 850 for 1992; 928 for 1993; 919 for 1994

	1992		1993		1994	
	Coeff.	t-stat.	Coeff.	t-stat.	Coeff.	t-stat.
Constant	-0.01	-0.67	0.08	8.28	-0.00	-0.08
Profit/sales	-0.38	-1.46	-0.39	-2.82	0.34	3.10
Losses/sales	0.40	4.61	0.28	4.46	0.78	8.62
Credit/sales	-0.16	-5.00	0.02	1.02	0.04	1.90
Receivables/sales	1.47	13.78	0.49	9.02	0.85	19.30

Source: Polish Statistical Office, 3-digit dataset provided to the author

bank credit. In Hungary in 1992, payables were more than twice as large as short-term bank credit to enterprises. In both countries trade credit is much more widely used than bank credit. Ranking firms by size of payables, one finds similar proportions for sales and payables for Poland (table 2.9). This holds for both state and

Table 2.11

Hungary: Trade Credit 1989-93

(a)   State firms

Dependent variable: payables as a share of sales

Variable	1989		1990		1991		1992		1993	
	Coeff.	t-stat.	Coeff.	t-stat.	Coeff.	t-stat.	Coeff.	t-stat.	Coeff.	t-stat.
Constant	0.01	1.68	0.07	16.56	0.06	13.23	0.02	6.77	0.03	4.28
Profit/sales	0.25	8.02	-0.41	-21.53	-0.33	-21.81	-0.05	-5.49	-0.14	-5.12
Short-term Bank credit /sales	-0.01	-0.19	-0.06	-1.57	-0.01	-0.28	0.02	0.67	0.03	1.01
Long-term Bank credit /sales	n.a.	n.a.	-0.13	-3.29	-0.16	-4.60	0.02	0.55	-0.01	-0.16
Receivables/ sales	0.67	30.13	0.51	27.65	0.62	33.59	0.53	31.92	0.46	18.71

(b)   Private firms

Dependent variable: payables as a share of sales

Variable	1989		1990		1991		1992		1993	
	Coeff.	t-stat	Coeff.	t-stat.	Coeff.	t-stat.	Coeff.	t-stat.	Coeff.	t-stat.
Constant	0.07	8.91	0.10	25.27	0.10	34.23	0.06	4.60	0.05	5.60
Profit/sales	0.28	10.90	-0.12	-18.34	-0.19	-29.18	-0.04	-14.96	0.03	2.58
Short-term Bank credit/ sales	0.12	3.31	0.08	4.56	0.02	1.58	0.15	13.37	0.24	8.42
Long-term Bank credit/ sales	n.a.	n.a.	0.06	2.58	0.05	2.59	0.02	1.14	0.15	3.45
Receivables/ sales	0.50	22.66	0.57	42.17	0.53	45.52	0.73	76.26	0.41	9.58

private firms. For Poland, regressions on trade credit (payables divided by sales) confirm the importance of the "circular model" emphasized by Calvo and Coricelli (1994) (table 2.10).

Indeed, receivables seem to be a key variable affecting payables. However, the profitability of firms plays a fundamental role, with high ratios of payables absorbed by firms with low profitability or losses. One can conclude that the transaction motive is dominant in the trade credit market, although there is also an important transfer of liquidity from liquidity-rich (profitable) firms to liquidity-poor firms. Interestingly, and this confirms results obtained on time series, the correlation between bank credit and payables is positive, although the coefficient is not statistically significant. A distinct regression for the subset of private firms indicates that ownership does not matter in the trade credit market, as the coefficients for private firms are analogous to those derived for the whole sample. Thus, private trade credit markets played a crucial role in financing the operations of enterprises. It is worth noting that private firms and small- and medium-sized firms used trade credit extensively to finance their operations, as an alternative to bank credit.

Results for Hungary broadly confirm those obtained for Poland. Table 2.11 summarizes the results of cross-section regressions on Hungarian firms during the period 1989–93. Again, the robust result is that the ratio of payables to sales will be higher, the higher the ratio of receivables to sales.

Summing up, the role of banks as engine of change in successful transition economies probably has been exaggerated (see van Wijnbergen 1994, and Pinto and van Wijnbergen 1995 for a different view). A distinguishing feature of successful PCPEs was the development of a well-functioning trade credit market. This suggests that, in addition to macroeconomic stability, these countries could rely on effective market institutions, broadly defined to include the rules of the game in addition to behavioral rules. We conjecture that in countries such as Hungary and Poland there was a learning period during the phase of partial reforms of the 1970s and 1980s (see Murrell 1995 for a similar argument). The experience with decentralized transactions and marketlike behaviors in the prereform period helped to prepare the ground for market development after full-fledged reforms. Lacking these prerequisites, the application of market reforms can lead to the development of dysfunctional institutions.[12]

Even in one of the most advanced countries in transition, Poland, the discipline of the financial sector on loss-making enterprises proved difficult. The implementation of the bank restructuring scheme of 1993 (see Anderson, Berglof, and Mizei 1996) yielded a significant decline in arrears toward banks. However, this took place at the expense of an increase in interenterprise and tax arrears (Grosfeld 1994). Loss-making firms, which accounted for practically all arrears to banks, were thus financed mainly through arrears to the budget. In net terms, interenterprise arrears represented a much smaller source of financing (table 2.12). Arrears to banks were much less relevant. The important finding is that through tax arrears, loss-making firms were able to repay a larger proportion of bank credit. A striking fact concerning the financing of state firms is that the sum of arrears to the government and to other enterprises was higher than the stock of bank credit to enterprises. Thus, a large proportion of financing for state firms came from involuntary credit and implicit subsidies. The so-called "decentralized" Polish model de facto involved a large role for government transfers to enterprises. Table 2.12 also shows a dramatically different behavior by private firms, with default in payment to the budget and to other enterprises much smaller than those of state firms.

Table 2.12

Poland: Financing Loss-Making Firms: Net Losses and Arrears, in Percent of Sales

	Net losses	Arrears with banks	Tax arrears	Interenterprise arrears*	Total arrears
1992					
State	-18	3	12	9	24
Private	-7	4	2	2	9
1993					
State	-15	3	13	11	27
Private	-1	1	1	0	2
1994					
State	-9	3	12	8	23
Private	-6	3	2	2	7

* Overdue payables. However, on a net basis (overdue payables minus overdue receivables), loss-making industrial firms have a roughly balanced position with other firms.

Source: Polish Statistical Office, 3-digit dataset provided to the author

The next section uses these arguments to explain the sharply different outcomes in the financial sector that characterized various PCPEs. The focus is on interenterprise arrears.

6.3 Development of Markets versus Development of Dysfunctional Institutions: Interenterprise Arrears and Monetary Policy

Interenterprise arrears have been an important phenomenon in the early stages of transition. In some countries, such as Romania and Russia, they have been a major stumbling block in the reform process (Ickes and Ryterman 1993; Calvo and Coricelli 1994; Clifton and Kahn 1993; Rostowski 1993). Potentially good and bad firms were intertwined in a chain of arrears threatening to cause a financial collapse of the economy. The attempt of the government to "clean" the worrying chain of arrears by injecting bank credit coincided with a fundamental loss of credibility of the stabilization programs. Interestingly, in other reforming economies (Hungary, Poland, and former Czechoslovakia) arrears, while present, did not grow into a systemic problem.

Several interpretations of the explosion of arrears and of the heterogeneity of country experiences have been put forward. To simplify, three groups of explanations may be identified. First, there is the view that arrears reflect a sort of continuation of soft budget constraints, with inefficient firms absorbing liquidity from more efficient firms. A corollary of this interpretation is that at the root of the phenomenon there is a credit policy that is too soft. A credible policy of tight credit would have avoided the explosion of arrears (Rostowski 1993). A second, more optimistic, explanation considers the phenomenon of arrears as a natural tendency toward a market for trade credit, which plays an important role in market economies (Begg and Portes 1993). A third view, which we favor, argues that the explosion of arrears reflects a systemic phenomenon which, in response to a liquidity squeeze, yields an equilibrium characterized by a generalized default on interenterprise payments. Such equilibrium is likely to be inefficient, as arrears are a form of involuntary lending that involves costs similar to those associated with shirking and stealing in market economies (Calvo and Coricelli 1994). Each of the above views implies different features of arrears and different remedies.

Whatever the interpretation chosen, it is unquestionable that the phenomenon of arrears offers an important perspective on the reform process in PCPEs, on the effects of policies, and on the interaction between macroeconomic policies and structural and institutional aspects of economies in transition. In particular, the study of arrears may shed light on the process of *creation of a market,* with its attendant set of incentives, penalties, and enforcement rules. Moreover, it is argued that in this process of market creation, *dysfunctional* institutions and modes of behavior may emerge. Interenterprise arrears may in fact be an example of such dysfunctional market.

6.3.1 Arrears: Main Developments

As illustrated in Calvo and Coricelli (1993), all stabilization programs in PCPEs—with the exception of Hungary and the former Yugoslavia in 1990—implied a sharp fall in the effective supply of bank credit. The fact that interenterprise arrears invariably increased in relation to bank credit at the outset of stabilization programs may be interpreted as an indication of the tightening of bank credit. Indeed, if the drop in real bank credit simply reflected the drop in output—caused by exogenous forces—one would have expected interenterprise credit to fall proportionally with respect to bank credit. However, country experiences were highly heterogeneous (Calvo and Coricelli 1994). This heterogeneity cannot be simply related to different magnitudes of the initial contraction in bank credit.

In particular, after the launching of stabilization programs interenterprise arrears exploded in some countries, such as Romania and Russia, but not in other PCPEs, such as Poland and Hungary. Moreover, in both Romania and Russia the explosion of arrears was accompanied by a general bail-out operation. Countries that experienced an explosion of arrears did also experience high and persistent inflation. The experience of the former Czechoslovakia is a sort of outlier, as arrears grew rapidly despite a stable macroeconomic environment.

Important differences across countries relate not only to the magnitude of arrears, but also to their characteristics. In Hungary and Poland, as in the former Yugoslavia, there was a system of trade credit in the prereform period. Arrears were just a proportion of this trade credit, about 30 percent. Thus, interenterprise arrears represent the nonperforming component of a largely voluntary trade credit system.[13]

By contrast, in Romania, Russia, and Ukraine, there was no developed system of trade credit. Arrears were the main, albeit special, form of involuntary trade credit. This difference points to the importance of institutional aspects concerning the development of private credit markets. In this respect, while a failure in most aspects, the experience of partial reforms carried out in Hungary and Poland before 1990 has proved important in laying down the basic structure of market institutions.

Another feature of interenterprise arrears worth emphasizing is that a large proportion is indeed associated with firms that have roughly similar payable and receivable arrears. In both the former Czechoslovakia, Poland, Romania, and Ukraine—the countries for which information is available—net arrears account for about 30 percent of gross arrears. Thus, a large proportion of arrears do not imply any net transfer of liquidity among firms.[14]

Finally, the comparison between the behavior of state and private firms in relation to the interenterprise credit market would shed some light on the role of microeconomic incentives. In this regard, we have only some information on Poland, which nevertheless points to the clearly different role played by interenterprise arrears in the two types of firms. In particular, in 1992 the ratio of overdue payables to sales in private firms was just one-third of that for state firms (2.8 percent against 10 percent).

This brief overview raises three central sets of issues that any explanation of interenterprise credit in PCPEs must tackle. First, experience shows a high degree of heterogeneity across countries. There are different possible outcomes of an initial credit squeeze, as arrears exploded only in Romania and Russia but not in other countries. Second, an explanation is needed for why a network of arrears can persist in a context of decentralized decisions by firms. Finally, one should be able to account for the fact that the network of arrears is highly circular, with firms having similar amounts of arrears on both sides of their balance sheet. The model developed in Calvo and Coricelli (1994) reviewed in section 4.6 above is a first attempt at explaining these features.

Table 2.13

Interenterprise Arrears and Arrears to Banks: Poland

(a) Interenterprise Arrears: All industrial firms

Dependent variable: Overdue payables/sales
Tobit estimation. Observations: 1135 for 1992; 1116 for 1993; 1140 for 1994

	1992		1993		1994	
	Coeff.	t-stat.	Coeff.	t-stat.	Coeff.	t-stat.
Constant	-0.02	-5.17	-0.02	-3.95	-0.02	-14.80
Profit/sales	-0.17	-2.29	-0.15	-1.87	-0.01	-0.90
Losses/sales	0.38	19.76	0.23	11.03	-0.03	-2.53
Bank Credit/sales	-0.12	-11.47	-0.01	-0.90	0.03	1.67
Arrears receivables/sales	0.88	19.27	0.46	9.90	0.99	62.76

(b) Interenterprise Arrears: Private firms

Dependent variable: Overdue payables/sales
Tobit estimation. Observations: 850 for 1992; 928 for 1993; 919 for 1994

	1992		1993		1994	
	Coeff.	t-stat.	Coeff.	t-stat.	Coeff.	t-stat.
Constant	-0.02	-4.18	-0.00	-2.70	-0.01	-10.68
Profit/sales	-0.13	-1.99	-0.10	-1.86	-0.03	-1.54
Losses/sales	0.34	14.68	0.06	2.39	-0.02	-2.01
Bank Credit/sales	-0.12	-11.52	0.00	0.40	-0.00	-0.12
Arrears receivables/sales	0.73	14.13	0.35	8.03	1.02	68.78

(c) Arrears to Banks: All industrial firms

Dependent variable: Overdue repayments to banks/sales
Tobit estimation. Observations: 1135 for 1992; 1116 for 1993; 1140 for 1994

	1992		1993		1994	
	Coeff.	t-stat.	Coeff.	t-stat.	Coeff.	t-stat.
Constant	-0.23	-10.02	-0.14	-5.72	-0.38	-7.28
Profit/sales	-0.13	-1.27	-0.97	-3.10	0.43	2.35
Losses/sales	0.34	13.90	0.26	5.21	1.29	8.30
Ownership dummy*	-0.12	-0.24	-0.06	-2.58	-0.17	-3.29

* 1 for private firms, 0 for state firms

Table 2.14

Romania: Interenterprise Arrears, 1992

Dependent variable: Overdue payables/sales
Tobit estimation

Variable	Coefficient	T-statistics
Constant	0.28	1.77
Material/total costs	0.18	6.98
Profits/sales	-0.51	-7.90
Exports/sales	0.00	0.02
Receivables/sales	0.35	21.61

6.3.2 The Chain of Arrears

Let us first define two important concepts, those of *net* and *gross* arrears. Arrears involve a bilateral relationship between two firms: for each debt there is a corresponding credit. If we aggregate arrears over the whole universe of firms involved, they of course add up to zero. In the aggregate, net arrears are zero. However, we can define net arrears as the sum of debts of all firms having a net debt position. For instance, assume there are three firms. Firm A has debts for 10 and credit for 5 (net debt of 5); firm B, as firm A, has debts for 10 and credit for 5 (net debt of 5). The last firm, firm C, must have debts for 10 (equal to the sum of credits of A and B) and credits for 20 (sum of debts of A and B), thus it has a net credit position of 10. If we add net debts and credits of the three firms, the total is zero. However, if we add only the value of net debts of the debtor firms, we obtain net debts for 10. Why is this 10 relevant? It is relevant because it indicates the liquidity flow from liquidity-rich to liquidity-poor firms. If debtors never repay their debts, there is a transfer of 10 to the debtors from firm C. Gross arrears are simply the sum of all debts, 30 in our example.

6.3.3 Analysis of Microeconomic Data: Poland, Romania, and Russia

The analysis of aggregate data has shown that the phenomenon of arrears has been a fundamental by-product of stabilization programs. Moreover, the phenomenon has been sharply heterogenous across countries, both in terms of the magnitude of the arrears and—even more importantly—of the characteristics of

Table 2.15a

Interenterprise Arrears in Russia: Regressions on Enterprise Data

(a) Overdue payables

Dependent variable: Overdue payables (scaled by employment)
Observations: 171
OLS regression

Variable	Coefficient	t-statistics
Overdue receivables/employment	0.21	5.63
Bank liabilities	-1.34	-3.18
SEC1	3.89	4.68
SEC2	2.16	3.89
SEC3	1.24	1.31
SEC4	0.54	0.98
SEC5	1.46	3.61
SEC6	0.81	2.16
SEC7	0.76	1.23
SEC8	0.63	1.23
SEC9	1.01	1.66
SEC10	0.76	1.89
SEC11	0.67	0.93
SEC12	1.46	1.90
SEC13	1.42	2.02
SEC14	0.83	1.07
SEC15	0.59	1.14
SEC16	0.83	1.78
SEC17	0.57	0.84
SEC19	1.19	2.60
SEC20	0.79	2.09
SEC21	0.90	2.33
SEC22	0.84	1.93
SEC23	1.97	3.45
SEC24	1.25	2.35
SEC25	0.15	0.16

Adjusted R-squared: 0.37

Table 2.15b

Interenterprise Arrears in Russia: Regressions on Enterprise Data

(b) Non-overdue payables

Dependent variable: Non-overdue payables/employment
Number of observations: 175
OLS regression

Variable	Coefficient	t-statistics
Non-overdue receivables/employment	0.08	0.45
Bank liabilities	-1.52	-1.12
SEC1	2.74	1.10
SEC2	8.51	5.21
SEC3	0.60	0.19
SEC4	0.33	0.19
SEC5	1.60	1.25
SEC6	0.66	0.55
SEC7	0.75	0.37
SEC8	0.72	0.43
SEC9	0.97	0.49
SEC10	0.64	0.49
SEC11	1.03	0.47
SEC12	0.43	0.17
SEC13	0.55	0.25
SEC14	0.80	0.35
SEC15	0.62	0.39
SEC16	0.85	0.56
SEC17	0.65	0.30
SEC18	1.52	0.33
SEC19	0.73	0.49
SEC20	0.88	0.72
SEC21	0.70	0.56
SEC22	0.80	0.56
SEC23	2.06	1.16
SEC24	1.44	0.84
SEC25	0.33	0.11

Adjusted R-squared: 0.000626

Table 2.16

Romania: Main Determinants of Interenterprise Arrears: Enterprise Survey

Accumulation of overdue payables	2.65
High interest rates	3.52
Increase in input over output prices	3.66
High profit tax	4.69
Loss of markets	5.38
Inventory accumulation	5.66
High turnover tax	5.66
Insufficient bank credit	5.76
High wage bill	7.86

Note: On a scale of 1 to 10, the lower the rating, the more important is the cause.

Source: World Bank, "Fiscal study on Romania," (1993).

arrears. In order to address the issue of the interaction between macroeconomic policies and enterprise adjustment—broadly, the issue of soft budget constraints—we have carried out microeconomic analyses for Romania, Poland and Russia.[15] The regression analysis suggests that for all countries the hypothesis of a chain of arrears is supported by the data. Tables 2.13 to 2.15 summarize the results of regressions on Poland, Romania and Russia.

Five main points stand out from the regressions on Poland.

(1.) Even when controlling for a host of variables describing the characteristics of firms, arrears in receivables emerge as a key explanatory variable for arrears in payables.

(2.) Liquidity constraints, proxied by profitability, tend to be associated with higher arrears.

(3.) The role of institutional factors is highlighted by the negative impact on arrears of the integration with foreign markets (proxied by the export/sales ratio). Thus, it seems that the chain of arrears relates to a domestic system of rules of the game. Reliance on foreign markets allows firms to escape the chain.

(4.) Such technological factors as the nonlabor input intensity of production (proxied by the share of material costs in total costs) appear significant.

(5.) Ownership does not affect the determinants of arrears once a firm has defaulted. However, state firms in Poland are much more likely to default on payments to other firms than are private enterprises.

In Romania results confirm the dominant role of unpaid receivables as determinant of overdue payables. Furthermore, results on Russian enterprises confirm the findings on Poland and Romania. Even after adjusting for sectoral dummies and other enterprise characteristics, a primary determinant of default on payments due is the default of the customers of the firm (unpaid receivables). This indicates the presence of a chain of arrears spreading into the system. Another important finding is that the nonoverdue payables, interpreted as normal trade credit, are not linked to receivables. Thus, normal credit operations may voluntarily involve the financing of transactions among firms, with credit channeled from liquidity-rich to liquidity-poor firms.

More qualitative indicators derived from survey results tend to confirm the view of a chain of arrears. Indeed, in Romania, when asked about the main cause of their own default on payments to suppliers, firms referred to the default on payments from their customers (table 2.16). The idea of the chain of arrears as a bad equilibrium induced by the interplay of a liquidity squeeze and unfavorable microeconomic incentives can be explored as well in a comparative perspective. Indeed, it is interesting to contrast the Romanian, Russian, and Ukrainian experiences with that of another economy in transition, Poland, which apparently did not suffer from the "disease" of a widespread chain of arrears.

As noted above, Poland displayed a fall in interenterprise arrears at the outset of stabilization. Thereafter, interenterprise credit remained at levels of similar, if not higher, magnitude to those for arrears in Romania. However, the characteristics were crucially different. Indeed, in Poland a market for voluntary credit developed and assisted the growth of activity of new entrants. In Romania, Russia, and Ukraine arrears spread into the system threatening the functioning of the economy, weakening the effectiveness of monetary policy, and ultimately contributing to maintaining the old production structure.

Summing up, the phenomenon of arrears has played an important role in the early stages of transformation of PCPEs. In some instances, arrears have crucially affected the overall course of reforms. The importance of arrears goes beyond their effects on monetary policy. Indeed, in economies in transition, arrears offer a perspective on the evolution of budget constraints and on the evolution of market institutions, namely, on how rapidly private markets can be introduced and what it takes for markets either to work efficiently or else to develop in a dysfunctional way.

3

Macroeconomic Constraints and Feedback

1. Introduction

Transition can be seen as a process of massive reallocation of resources across sectors and firms. Such a process contains elements of evolution—new firms emerge and absorb resources from the old, declining firms—and of policy design (firms are privatized, restructured, or closed by state intervention).[1] The dynamics of the economy crucially depend on the weight of these elements. The inherited economic structure and inherited capital stock play a fundamental role. How much of such capital can be used in the new market environment?[2] This chapter describes a simple model of transition and provides evidence for its empirical relevance.

The model we develop in this chapter illustrates the various transition paths that can emerge from different initial conditions in terms of human and physical capital stock. It appears that the less favorable the initial conditions are, the higher the unemployment cost of transition. There is a crucial trade-off between unemployment and overall restructuring of the economy. However, unemployment cannot be considered as an unconstrained variable. Indeed, there are fiscal and political economy effects of unemployment that can lead to a maximum tolerable rate of unemployment.

2. A Dynamic Framework: Multiple Adjustment Paths

Although it is a rough simplification, the adjustment following the initial output fall in economies in transition can be interpreted as the asymmetric dynamics of declining and growing sectors. Although the recovery of state firms deserves attention in some cases (most notably Poland), the distinction between private and state sectors captures a large part of the process.

2.1 Restructuring, Sectoral Reallocation, and Unemployment

Unemployment is likely to be associated with the process of restructuring. As the growing sector is small initially, the outflow of labor from the declining state sector is not fully matched by hirings in private firms, so that unemployment may arise during the process of reallocation of resources from state to private firms. That unemployment is an inevitable by-product of market reforms is unlikely to be controversial. However, more controversial is the role that unemployment plays during the transition. Even if one accepts the inevitability of a certain level of unemployment, the market may lead to rates of unemployment that are either too high or too low. Furthermore, it should be emphasized that the Czech Republic stands out as an exception to the view that associates unemployment with restructuring. Indeed, restructuring can be effected even with low unemployment.

2.1.1 The "Optimal Rate of Unemployment"

Assuming frictions in an equilibrium model of the labor market, it can be shown that decentralized equilibrium may be associated with an unemployment rate that is too high from a social-welfare point of view. Gavin (1993) illustrates a mechanism that is likely to have general validity. Consider an economy in which a significant proportion of the labor force must be reallocated across sectors, for instance, because of price/trade reform. Frictions in the labor market imply that the matching-up between job seekers and employers is not an instantaneous or costless process. It requires time. Part of this time is spent in the form of unemployment. As in typical search models, the higher the number of job seekers, the more likely it is that an employer will find the worker needed. However, for job seekers, the higher the number of unemployed, the lower the probability the single job seekers will find employment. Abstracting from the possibility of multiple equilibria or complicated dynamics, Gavin shows that in a two-sector model, there can be an excessive number of unemployed during the transition, as too many people leave the declining sector. The source of such inefficiency is that the individual worker decides to abandon the declining sector depending on the average rate of absorption by the growing sector. Indeed, the latter determines the probability of finding a job. However, from the social-welfare perspective it is the marginal rate of absorption that matters.

In a similar model, Burda (1993) derives the same conclusion through a different channel. The channel depends on macroeconomic constraints, namely fiscal constraints arising from unemployment. In the presence of a liquidity constraint for the government (a limit on the budget deficit at each point in time), unemployment has adverse effects on the economy through the financing of unemployment benefits with distortionary taxes. Although unemployment plays a positive role in facilitating restructuring in the economy, there is an optimal level of unemployment, beyond which welfare is reduced. In contrast, as shown in Chadha and Coricelli (1994), there is the opposite extreme of too low unemployment, that is, too low from the point of view of successful restructuring of the economy (although unclear from a social-welfare perspective).

It is worth noting that more successful reformers show higher rates of unemployment than unsuccessful, or lagging, countries.[3] However, as unemployment can also contain a short-term component linked to output behavior, a more informative indicator is the rate of unemployment in relation to the deviation of output from its full-employment level (for simplicity, the prereform level). Taking the prereform level of output as a starting point, the change in GDP represents a deviation from full employment. Dividing the rate of unemployment by the output index, it

Table 3.1

Ratio of Unemployment Rate and GDP Growth

	1989	1990	1991	1992	1993
Slow reformers	0.00	-0.10	-0.57	-0.47	-1.20
without Russia	0.00	-0.10	-0.57	-1.23	-8.31
Fast reformers	0.11	-0.69	-0.74	-2.30	-15.76

Source: EBRD (1995)

emerges even more clearly that successful reformers display a much higher ratio of unemployment, scaled by the behavior of output (table 3.1). The model developed below may account for these empirical phenomena.

3. A Model of Transition

The state sector is characterized by labor dominated firms. The coalition of workers maximizes the expected difference between its members' income and the alternative income if they were to leave the state sector. This alternative income is a weighted average of unemployment benefits and the private sector wage, with the weights given by the probability of remaining unemployed and the probability of obtaining a job in the private sector. Assuming risk neutrality, therefore a linear utility function of the workers, the objective function of the workers' coalition can be expressed as follows (as in Calvo 1978):

$$V_t^1 = L_t^1 \left[W_t^1 - (\delta_t B + (1 - \delta_t) W_t^2) \right] \tag{1}$$

where L^1 denotes employment in the state sector, W^1 the wage in the state sector, W^2 the wage in the private sector, and B unemployment benefits; δ represents the probability that a worker lai off from the state sector remains unemployed, and $(1 - \delta)$ represents the probability that he or she obtains employment in the private sector.

Production in the state sector is assumed to arise from a Cobb-Douglas production function, with labor as the only variable factor:

$$Q_t^1 = F(L_t^1) = (L_t^1)^\beta \quad \text{where } 0 < \beta < 1 \tag{2}$$

If workers appropriate all the revenues from the firm, wages will be equal to the average product of labor, net of the tax that the government can impose. In that case, the maximization of equation (1) is subject also to the zero profit condition:

$$(1 - \tau)PQ_t^1 - W_t^1 L_t^1 = 0 \tag{3}$$

where τ is the tax (or subsidy if negative) paid to the government and P is the price of the state-sector output expressed in terms of the private sector good, assumed as numeraire.

With a Cobb-Douglas production function, the average product of labor is just a multiple of the marginal product. If one assumes that wages are equal to the marginal product, labor does not change the results of the model. The movement of workers out of the state sector is determined by the following arbitrage condition:

$$W^1 = \left[\delta_t B + (1 - \delta_t) W_t^2 \right]$$

stating that workers will leave the state sector until the wage in that sector is equal to the expected alternative income. Using equation (3) to substitute for W^1, the following employment rule is obtained:

$$F'(L_t^1)^{\beta-1} = \frac{1}{\beta(1-\tau)P} \left[\delta_t B + (1 - \delta_t) W_t^2 \right] \tag{4}$$

Equation (4) states that employment in the state sector decreases with taxes, and with the probability of remaining unemployed, while it increases with the relative price, unemployment benefits, wages in the private sector, and with the probability of being employed in the private sector. In the state sector there is no investment in physical capital, no technological progress, and workers' effort is constant.

3.1 Private Sector

Output in the private sector is produced by a Cobb-Douglas technology, with labor (measured in efficiency units) and capital as production factors:

$$Q_t^2 = K_t^{1-\alpha} \left[E(W_t^2 - B, U_t) L_t^2 \right]^{\alpha} \tag{5}$$

where K denotes the capital stock and $E(.)$ the effort function, which is increasing in the premium of wages over unemployment benefits and in the rate of unemployment.

Profit maximization by the firm leads to the following conditions, from which wages and employment in the private sector can be derived:

$$\frac{\partial E(W_t^2 - B, U_t)}{\partial W_t^2} * \frac{W_t^2}{E(W_t^2 - B, U_t)} = 1 \qquad (6)$$

which is the so-called Solow condition, which implies that the elasticity of effort with respect to the real wage is unity. From that condition one can derive the following signs of derivatives:

$$\frac{\partial W_t^2}{\partial U_t} < 0 \quad \frac{\partial W_t^2}{\partial B} > 0$$

The level of employment in efficiency wage models is on the labor demand curve of the firm, which is

$$L_t^2 = \frac{[\alpha K_t]^{\frac{1}{1-\alpha}} [E(W_t^2 - B, U_t)]^{\frac{\alpha}{1-\alpha}}}{[W_t^2]^{\frac{1}{1-\alpha}}} \qquad (7)$$

Using (6), wages can be eliminated in (7) to obtain

$$L_t^2 = L^2[W^2(U_t; B), U_t, K_t, B] = L^2(U, K, B) \qquad (8)$$

with $\dfrac{\partial L^2}{\partial U} > 0 \quad \dfrac{\partial L^2}{\partial K} > 0 \quad \dfrac{\partial L^2}{\partial B} < 0$

3.2 Labor Market Equilibrium for a Given Capital Stock

Assuming that the private sector randomly selects workers from the pool of people who are not employed in the state sector, the probability that a worker abandoning the state sector becomes employed in the private sector is

91

$$1 - \delta_t = \frac{L_t^2}{L_t^2 + U_t} \tag{9}$$

Using (9) we can derive employment in the state sector as

$$L_t^1 = L^1(U_t, K_t; (1-\tau)P, B) \tag{10}$$

All the effects can be signed except those associated with a change in B, which has ambiguous effects on state-sector employment.

Equilibrium in the labor market requires that the sum of employed and unemployed people be equal to the labor force, which we normalize to be equal to one. Thus,

$$L^1(U, K, (1-\tau)P, B) + L^2(U, K, B) + U_t = 1 \tag{11}$$

Equation (11) yields a relationship between unemployment and the stock of capital (the UK curve).[4]

3.3 Private Sector Growth

Most papers on transition have emphasized the presence of adjustment costs, or search costs, in the labor market. Assuming a difference in the level of productivity in state and private sectors, they then derive results for the optimal speed of movement of labor from state to private firms. We emphasize explicitly that the forces affecting the growth of the private sector and the accumulation of capital, both human and physical, are the driving force of transition. To stress the central role of capital accumulation we abstract from the presence of adjustment or search costs in the labor market. Several models of investment, both in human and in physical capital, can be considered. Chadha and Coricelli (1995) and Chadha et al. (1993) analyze different models of investment. If one considers K in the production function of the private sector good as human capital or a generic technological factor that grows exogenously over time, transition takes place inevitably. Following Chadha et al. (1993), consider in equation (5) H_t in place of $K_t^{(1-\alpha)}$. Assume that H grows over time at a constant rate. This implies that total factor productivity in the private sector is continuously shifting over time. The system travels along the bell-shaped UK curve of figure 3.1. Economic policy can affect the shape of the curve, thus the level of unemployment during transition. However, whatever policies are implemented and whatever the initial level of human capital or technology, the economy eventually reaches its final equilibrium with all labor employed in the private sector.

Figure 3.1

Unemployment Dynamics

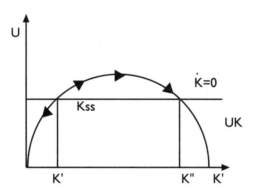

More interesting are the cases in which the process of growth of the private sector is endogenously determined. For instance, human capital can grow through a process of learning-by-doing. As in Lucas (1988), the growth of human capital is an increasing function of the number of workers employed in the private sector. Chadha et al. (1993) have shown that this implies the presence of two distinct equilibrium paths. The two paths are separated by a critical value of initial level of human capital in the private sector. The economy still travels along the *UK* curve. However, to the left of the critical value of human capital, transition fails and the economy gets stuck in an equilibrium dominated by state sector firms. In contrast, starting to the right of the critical value of human capital allows the economy to move toward specialization in the private sector good.

The case of investment in physical capital leads to similar, although richer, results. Chadha and Coricelli (1995) analyzed a model in which forward-looking firms in the private sector invest in physical capital. Investment takes place according to a standard, textbook-like specification (Blanchard and Fischer 1989). Firms maximize the present discounted value of profits, and investment is subject to installation costs. The resulting dynamics of the system display two steady-state equilibria, one with low capital and the other with high capital in the private sector. There is still a threshold level of initial capital to be used in the private sector that ensures transition will succeed. However, transition may crucially depend on expectations of private sector firms. Indeed, even when the initial capital stock would be sufficient to place the economy on a successful path, if expectations of future returns on investments are pessimistic, restructuring will not take place. Similarly, if expectations are optimistic, restructuring can take place even when the initial capital stock in the private sector is very low. Thus, transition does not depend only, in a deterministic fashion, on inherited capital, but it crucially depends on expectations. This implies that policies have an important effect through their impact on expectations. Another important aspect of the model is that initial conditions highlight a trade-off between the initial level of capital in the private sector and the rate of unemployment. Indeed, the lower the initial capital stock usable in the private sector, the higher the unemployment rate consistent with successful transition.

The presence of multiple equilibria and of a highly nonlinear adjustment path give an important role to economic policies. Two main policy issues stand out. One issue is that privatization policies can affect the initial stock of capital available to the private sector, and the other is that of the effects of fiscal policy and of fiscal constraints on restructuring and the speed of transition. Indeed, while several authors have identified the closure of state firms as the main policy instrument, one can argue that the indirect effects on the dynamics of state firms due to tax/subsidies appear to be more relevant.

3.4 Policy Intervention and the Speed of Transition: Privatization Policies and Fiscal Feedbacks

In the simple version of the model, we assumed that investment takes place only in private firms and that there is an initial capital stock in the private sector. However, a more realistic setting would consider the capital stock in the state sector and the possibility that the initial capital available for private firms can be determined by privatization.

3.4.1 The Extent of Privatization and the Speed of Transition

While privatization leads to higher output in the medium run, initially there may be an adverse effect as a fraction of the existing capital is likely to be lost (or "scrapped") during the privatization process. If this initial scrapping is not fully compensated by an immediate increase in total factor productivity associated with privatized firms, output and tax revenues decline, while unemployment and public expenditure increase. Thus, an interesting trade-off may arise between the speed of privatization, unemployment, and budgetary balance. We present simulations of the model sketched in section 2, modified to take privatization into account. Investment takes place in both sectors, and we assume that it depends on enterprise profits. The dynamics of the capital stock in state firms crucially depend on wage setting. If workers appropriate a share of profits larger than depreciation, "decapitalization" arises. Figure 3.2 reports the results of the simulation in terms of output and unemployment rates under different privatization programs. The results are quite striking. A more drastic privatization implies a fall in output and an increase in unemployment.

It is worth noting that in the initial phase, different privatization programs lead to sharply different rates of unemployment but rather similar output behavior. In relation to the analytical model, faster privatization may allow an economy with a very small private sector to move into the range of successful restructuring. Faster privatization implies that the turnaround of the economy occurs much earlier in the case of more ambitious privatization. A more moderate approach to privatization postpones the transfer of capital from the state to the private sector and keeps unemployment at a significantly lower level during the first few periods. The price to be paid for this temporary relief is a more severe recession and poorer growth performance later. This clearly implies that—other things being equal—the policymaker's choice between different privatization programs heavily depends on his horizon and time preference. Furthermore, there are important credibility issues.

When little privatization is undertaken, the trend in unemployment may continue to increase for a long time (see figure 3.2). At the same time, total output remains below its initial level, while tax rates increase. As a result, there is no obvious sign of recovery for an extended period of time. Given that the privatization program shows weak results, it is not likely to be credible

Figure 3.2

Endogenous Employment in the State Sector

Unemployment
with different speed of privatization (ks varying: lower
ks faster privatization)

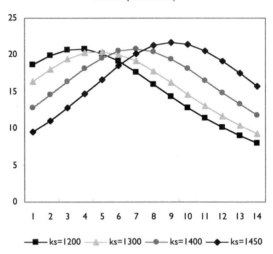

Private Sector Wages

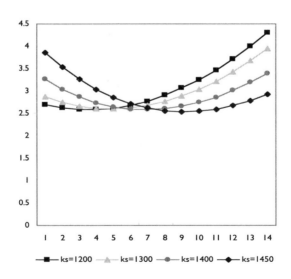

State Sector Wages

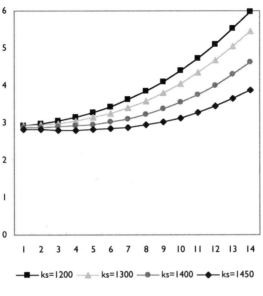

Total Output

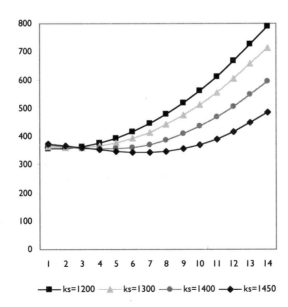

and thus may fail. An illustration of this effect in our model is to introduce the dependence of private sector investment on expected aggregate demand conditions (which can be characterized either by unemployment rates or by the level of total output). If the extent of privatization is small, private investors correctly forecast low levels of aggregate economic activity. This implies little investment and thus slower restructuring and a deeper crisis. Ultimately, unemployment may reach politically and socially unacceptable levels, and the transition process may come to a halt. By contrast, if privatization encompasses a larger share of state capital, the economy gets into the recovery phase very early. Expansionary expectations heightened through more investment contribute further to growth and speed up transition. Credibility problems are less likely to arise in this case. Thus, credibility considerations—other things being equal—call for more radical privatization measures. Notice, however, that the argument rests on the assumption that initial dislocation effects—the "scrapping" of state capital—are not too large. Moreover, faster privatization may imply extremely large adverse fiscal effects. The next section analyzes the role of fiscal constraints and fiscal policy on the transition path.

3.5 Fiscal Constraints and the Speed of Transition

Assuming that taxes are levied only on state firms, budget balance is simply the difference between tax revenues from state firms and unemployment benefits:

$$D_t = \tau P(L_t^1)^\beta - BU_t \tag{12}$$

Chadha and Coricelli (1994) show that the relationship between unemployment and the tax rate τ for a given budget balance is nonlinear and follows a hump-shaped curve. A second relationship can therefore be computed between unemployment and the tax rate from the labor market equilibrium condition (11). That relationship is monotonically increasing (see Chadha and Coricelli 1994). The effects of different constraints on the budget balance can be studied by shifting the two curves. The result is that when unemployment is high, tightening the budget constraints implies reducing taxation of state firms (or increasing subsidies to them).

Only when unemployment is low is tightening the budget consistent with higher taxation of state firms and thus with faster restructuring.

Before discussing in more detail the effects of budget tightening in the above model, let us review the issue in a more general context and in relation to different models.

4. A Medium-Term Perspective: Budget Deficit and Restructuring

While in the long run the movement to a market economy is bound to reduce the "size" of the government through contraction of expenditures and revenues, the transition is likely to affect revenues and expenditures asymmetrically. Fiscal imbalances are therefore likely to emerge. On the revenue side, the decline of the traditional base for tax revenue—state enterprises—produces a fall in revenues. On the expenditure side, social expenditures associated both with growing unemployment and with transfer of many "social" activities from enterprises to the government, produce upward pressure on total expenditures. We begin by discussing a mechanical example in which the dynamics of state and private sectors are exogenous.

4.1 A Mechanical (Accounting) Framework

It may be useful to start with a mechanical example in which the state sector declines at an exogenous rate, and the private sector expands at an exogenous rate (see also Hare 1994; Rodrik 1995). At the beginning of the transition, the distribution of the labor force is skewed towards state enterprises, so the decline in employment in state firms cannot be absorbed entirely by the initially small private sector. Unemployment therefore increases in the initial phases. After the private sector has reached a relevant size, unemployment begins to decline, so that the pattern of unemployment depicts a hump-shaped curve. The nonlinearity of the behavior of unemployment has important implications for the behavior of the budget deficit, which will in turn follow a U-shaped path. On the fiscal side, the basic assumptions are that tax revenue is raised primarily from state enterprises and that the government pays unemployment benefits. For simplicity, we assume that only state firms are taxed and that unemployment benefits are fixed.

99

Denote the labor force with N, employment in the state sector with E_s, employment in the private sector with E_p, and unemployment with U; the following identity holds at each point in time:

$$N = E_s + E_p + U \qquad (13)$$

For simplicity, the labor force is assumed to be constant and equal to 1, so the stock of unemployment is equivalent to the unemployment rate. Employment in the state sector declines at the constant rate d, while employment in the private sector grows at the constant rate g:

$$E_s(t) = E_s(0)e^{-dt} \qquad (14)$$

$$E_p(t) = E_p(0)e^{gt} \qquad (15)$$

At each point, unemployment is thus

$$U(t) = 1 - E_s(t) + E_p(t) = 1 - E_s(0)e^{-dt} - E_p(0)e^{gt} \qquad (16)$$

Differentiating the above expression with respect to time, we obtain the change of the rate of unemployment over time:

$$dU/dt = dE_s(0)e^{-dt} - gE_p(0)e^{gt} \qquad (17)$$

At $t = 0$,

$$dU/dt = dE_s(0) - gE_p(0) \qquad (18)$$

The typical initial conditions for the relative shares of state versus private employment in economies in transition were given by a share of the state sector close to one. Assume that before reforms 90 percent of workers were employed in the state sector. The decline of state employment during the first year of transition was around 10 percent in Central and Eastern European countries. In order to avoid an increase in unemployment, the rate of growth of the private sector should have been about 1,000 percent. To illustrate the dynamics of unemployment and the budget deficit, we assume that $d = g$.

If the share of employment in the state sector is initially larger than that in the private sector, which is the relevant case for economies in transition,

$$dU/dt = d(E_s(0) - E_p(0)) > 0 \qquad (19)$$

If t is sufficiently large, unemployment will decline:

$$dU/dt = d(Es(0)e^{-dt} - E_p(0)e^{dt}) < 0 \qquad (20)$$

Assume unemployment benefits per unemployed person are constant and equal to b; moreover, assume that unemployment benefits are the only expenditure for the government. Thus

$$G = bU \qquad (21)$$

Revenues are obtained by taxing output of state and private firms:

$$T = \tau_s f(E_s) + \tau_p f(E_p) \qquad (22)$$

The budget deficit is thus

$$D = bU - [\tau_s f(E_s) + \tau_p f(E_p)] \qquad (23)$$

For given tax rates, the budget deficit deteriorates during the initial phases as unemployment increases. The deterioration is more significant if tax rates differ, namely, are higher on state firms, as is the case in economies in transition. Figure 3.3 illustrates the behavior of the budget and of unemployment over time. The result from this example is simply that, ceteris paribus, the budget deficit is bound to deteriorate during the process of transition as a by-product of the reallocation of resources from the state to the private sector.

The usefulness of this mechanical example is to show that if a main feature of the transition is the reallocation of resources from state to private firms, then unemployment will generally follow a hump-shaped path, irrespective of the specific model cho-

Figure 3.3

Unemployment and Budget Deficit

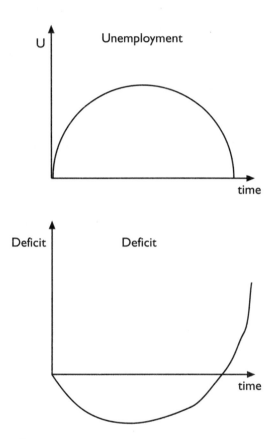

sen for the labor market. Of course, a mechanical model cannot shed light on the important behavioral feedbacks that affect the response of both state and private sectors to fiscal variables and so cannot serve as a guide to policy. The next section briefly outlines a framework highlighting these feedbacks.

4.2 Feedbacks: Endogenous Adjustment of State and Private Firms

Several observers have stressed the importance of the fiscal implications of unemployment for the pace of restructuring, defined as reallocation of resources from state to private firms.[5] As noted in the previous section, the behavior of unemployment and the budget crucially depends upon the speed at which the state sector declines when compared to the speed at which the private sector expands.

Aghion and Blanchard (1993) focused on the effects of budget constraints on the growth of the private sector. They stressed the presence of a "fiscal externality" which can lead to multiple equilibria, one with high unemployment and no private sector growth, and one with low unemployment and expansion of the private sector. In their models the growth of the private sector (that is, private sector hiring) is an increasing function of the rate of unemployment. This can be due to either an easier match-up between job seekers and job offers, or to unemployment's downward pressure on wages, which leads to more hirings in the private sector. However, through the fiscal channel, unemployment may have an adverse effect on the growth of the private sector, which through higher taxes bears the cost of unemployment. The presence of these two conflicting forces can lead to two equilibria. Indeed, if the growth of the private sector is rapid, the tax burden to finance unemployment expenditures is low and does not hamper the growth of the private sector. By contrast, if the growth of the private sector is slow, the burden of unemployment is high, and tax pressure is an obstacle to private sector growth.

Note that private firms are likely to be forward looking in their investment and hiring decisions. What matters for them is the flow of taxes raised over the entire life of their activity. Box 3.1 summarizes the main behavioral relations of the simplest version of the model.

Deficit financing simply modifies the government budget constraint by adding a constant term to the right-hand side:

$$bU = z\,(1\text{-}U) + d,$$

where d is the budget deficit. It is easy to show that a positive d (a budget deficit) shifts the curve $f(U)$ upward.

This has one simple but interesting implication. Deficit financing increases the feasible rate of closure of the state sector. The feasible rate is given by the rate consistent with an ss line tangent to the maximum of the $f(U)$ curve. In figure 3.4b, the line ss would not be consistent with equilibrium in the model with no

Box 3.1
Aghion and Blanchard Model

The state sector declines at a constant rate s (constant flow of exit from state firms). Denoting E for employment in the state sector:

$$dE/dt = -s$$

The private sector is populated by firms that set wages according to an efficiency wage mechanism and "invest" in new jobs, taking into account the present discounted value of profits. Denoting V as the value of a new private job and N as employment in the private sector:

$$dN/dt = arV$$

$$rV = (y-w-z) + dV/dt$$

where r is the rate of interest, y the constant marginal product of labor, w the wage rate and z the tax rate. From standard efficiency wage considerations the following wage rule is derived:

$$w = b + c\,(r+H/U)$$

where b is unemployment benefits, H is the hiring rate in the private sector, and U the unemployment pool. To these basic equations Aghion and Blanchard add a government budget constraint:

$$Ub = (1 - U)\,z$$

The model can be solved in the V-U space, obtaining a bell-shaped curve for the locus of points consistent with $dV/dt = 0$; the curve for $dU/dt = 0$ is a straight line intersecting the y-axis at $V= s/ar$ (figure 3.4).

Figure 3.4

Aghion and Blanchard Model

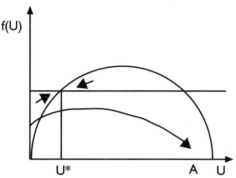

Aghion and Blanchard Model with Deficit Financing

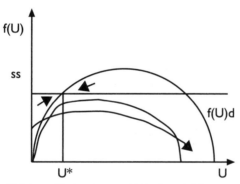

f(U)d=equilibrium locus with budget deficit

deficit, but it is consistent (intersects the new curve $f(U)'$) with equilibrium with deficit financing. Thus, a budget deficit permits a faster rate of restructuring of the economy, or, to put it differently, a too-tight budget constraint implies a slower pace of restructuring.[6] However, the result must be qualified. Indeed, the Aghion-Blanchard model displays multiple equilibrium paths. In the relevant region of initial conditions to the left of U^*, in addition to the path converging to a long-run equilibrium with successful restructuring (development of the private sector), there is a path leading to high unemployment and failed restructuring (point *A* in figure 3.4). Expectations play a crucial role for the selection of the actual equilibrium path.

In order to assess the effects of deficit financing, the impact of the deficit on expectations must be taken into account. For a given *s*, deficit financing implies a lower level of unemployment. It can be argued that this may affect expectations positively, increasing the likelihood of the "optimistic" path. On the other hand, if deficit financing is associated with higher inflation, the conjecture can be reversed, as the likelihood of the "pessimistic" path may increase.

To sum up, the model implies that relaxing the budget constraint may permit a faster restructuring of the economy. However, loosening the budget constraint is not a sufficient condition for a successful restructuring, as the final outcome depends upon the expectations of the actors in the economy.[7] Thus, the following section discusses a different model, in which restructuring may slow down as an endogenous response to tight budget constraints.

4.3 Fiscal Constraints and Incentives to Slow Down Transition

Borrowing the model of Chadha and Coricelli (1994), we sketch a framework that contains three main features. First, in the model, unemployment is not simply a by-product of restructuring but plays a crucial role in determining the restructuring process. Second, the model endogenizes the behavior of the state sector in relation to fiscal variables. Third, to make the analysis of transition interesting, the restructuring process does not take place "naturally" but requires accumulation of resources in the private sector, for instance, physical and/or human capital. As in Aghion and Blanchard (1993), the success of the restructuring process is not inevitable. However, different from their study, there is a threshold combination of unemployment and technological capabilities— human or physical capital—that separates a region of successful restructuring from one of failed restructuring. For a given initial endowment of technological capabilities, there is a threshold level of unemployment necessary for restructuring to succeed. Since unemployment is costly for the budget, the threshold level of unemployment implies a budget deficit. If the government faces strict borrowing constraints and/or a ceiling on the budget deficit—for instance, as part of the stabilization package—it has the incentive to adopt policies that reduce the level of unemployment. This reduction implies in turn a slowdown of restructuring and may jeopardize the eventual success of restructuring.

Figures 3.5 to 3.8 illustrate the behavior of the system and its response to different degrees of fiscal constraints and to various policy changes. The model assumes that only the state sector is taxed. Recall from section 2 that the model yields a nonmonotonic relationship between unemployment and the stock of capital invested in the private sector. Unemployment continues to grow during the transition before it declines. The decline begins well after the output in the economy has begun to increase. Thus, the model seems to account for the weak correlation between output changes and unemployment discussed in section 5 below. The dynamics of unemployment can follow two distinct paths, as illustrated in figure 3.1 above. One leads to successful restructuring, with the economy eventually specializing in the private sector. The other implies a failed restructuring: the private sector does not take off, and the economy is dominated by the state sector. There is a critical level of capital stock in the private sector that separates the two different paths. The behavior of the budget deficit differs along the two paths (figure 3.5). In the case of failed restructuring the budget balance improves over time. In the case

Figure 3.5

Budget Balance Along Successful and Failed

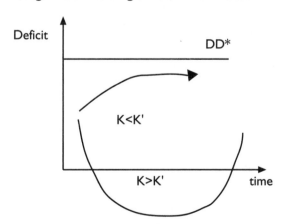

*Deficit for unemployment=0, and all labor employed in private sector

Figure 3.6

Effects of Budget Deficits

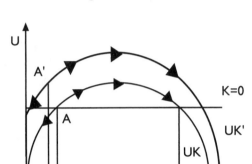

of successful restructuring, the budget deteriorates before it improves, mirroring the behavior of unemployment. The model provides analytical foundations for the warning advanced by Tanzi (1993) and Kornai (1993) on the low informational value of budget deficits in economies in transition.

As in the Aghion and Blanchard model, a loosening of the budget constraint increases the likelihood of successful restructuring. Indeed, as shown in figure 3.6, higher deficits enlarge the interval of initial conditions on the capital stock consistent with convergence to the "good" equilibrium. A crucial difference from the Aghion-Blanchard model is that in the Chadha and Coricelli model less restrictive budget constraints lead to higher unemployment and an endogenous increase in the speed of restructuring. The source of the difference is that in the Chadha and Coricelli model, loosening of the budget constraint permits higher tax pressure on state firms, rather than a reduction of taxes, as in the Aghion-Blanchard model (figure 3.7).

The higher tax pressure increases the speed of reallocation of labor from state to private firms. This feature of the model is consistent with the empirical observations presented in section 5.2, which indicate a higher fiscal pressure on state firms in the group of "fast" reformers, together with higher rates of unemployment in relation to output dynamics. Note that this result is only one of the two possible outcomes in the model. Indeed, the result

Figure 3.7

Taxes and Government Budget Constraints:
Effects of Tightening the Budget

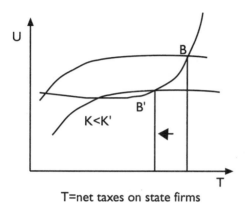

T=net taxes on state firms

arises when unemployment is sufficiently high and thus has important budgetary implications. For low levels of unemployment, loosening the budget constraint is consistent with lower taxation of state firms.

If we interpret the results from the perspective of a tightening of the budget constraint, the model provides an explanation for the slowdown of restructuring that has been observed in several countries a few years into the transition process. Such a slowdown can be rationalized as a response to fiscal constraints that become tighter as transition progresses and induce governments to reduce fiscal pressure on state firms. In addition to the incentives to modify the pace of restructuring, the model can be used to analyze several policy measures.

4.4 Policy Analysis

Several policies can be discussed using the above models. Let us start with tax and subsidy measures.

(1.) Wage and employment subsidies to state firms have an adverse effect on restructuring. Since subsidies can be considered as negative taxation, the analysis of their impact on transition coincides with the analysis carried out above for the case of taxation of state firms. Wage subsidies reduce unemployment and improve the budget in the short run, but slow down transition.

(2.) Wage subsidies for hirings in private firms improve the prospects for successful transition. However, they exert pressure on the budget in the short run. Fiscal constraints therefore may limit the use of this instrument. "Active" policies can be effective in speeding up the pace of transition, but they involve significant short-term fiscal costs.

Figure 3.8

Effects of Unemployment Benefits

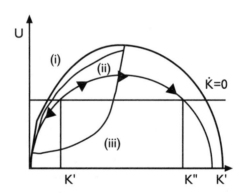

(3.) The effects of *unemployment benefits* are less trivial. The impact of changes in such benefits on the dynamics of unemployment is ambiguous. Either of two cases may arise. The first, an upward shift of the *UK* curve, implies higher unemployment and increases the probability of successful transition (figure 3.8). The second case involves a period of reduced unemployment and has an adverse effect on the process of restructuring. Box 3.2 summarizes the various effects that contribute to make the overall effect indeterminate.

Box 3.2

Effects of Unemployment Benefits on Unemployment and the Budget Deficit

The effects of changes in unemployment benefits B on unemployment and the budget are ambiguous because there are four channels through which they may work. The ambiguity arises from the uncertain impact of an increase in B on state sector employment. By increasing the reservation wage, higher B would tend to decrease employment in state firms (L'). However, higher B implies lower job creation in private firms, reducing the probability of workers becoming employed in that sector. If this second effect dominates, L' may increase and unemployment decrease. The effect on the budget can be decomposed in the following four expressions:

$$\frac{dD}{dB} = -U - B\frac{dU}{dB} + \tau A\frac{\partial L'}{\partial B} + \tau A\frac{\partial L'}{\partial U}\frac{dU}{dB}$$

where τ is the tax rate on state output and A is an expression including employment in the state sector and other parameters of the model.

The four channels are:

(1.) direct impact of unemployment on the budget;

(2.) impact through the change in unemployment;

(3.) impact through the outflow from the state sector (reduction of the tax base);

(4.) impact of the outflow from the state sector through its impact on higher unemployment.

Both (dU/dB) and (dL'/dB) have uncertain signs. Depending on their signs three cases are possible:

(1.) $(dU/dB)>0, (dL'/dB)<0$

(2.) $(dU/dB)>0, (dL'/dB)>0$

(3.) $(dU/dB)<0, (dL'/dB)>0$

Cases/Channels

Combinations	1	2	3	4
(1.)	-	-	-	+
(2.)	-	-	+	+
(3.)	-	+	+	-

If we consider also the effects on the budget, three cases can be distinguished (figure 3.8). They are associated with different signs of the four channels affecting the impact on the budget balance. Cases one and two have favorable effects on restructuring, while the third has a negative effect on restructuring. All have ambiguous effects on the budget. Of course, the rationale for a policy of high benefits is strong in the first two cases, wherein the budget balance improves. Independent of the effect on the budget, the third case has an adverse effect on restructuring that by itself reduces the attractiveness of that policy. Taking the simple structure of the model into account, the various outcomes are simply suggestive.

It is important that in the model, policies that increase unemployment in the initial stages of transition exert a positive effect on restructuring. Unemployment benefits are one example of such policies. Their attractiveness derives from the fact that high benefits work as incentives for workers to leave the state sector. However, the above discussion highlights the risks of such a policy. Indeed, high benefits may lead to very bad outcomes, even though they might, under certain circumstances, improve the chances of successful transition. What the model suggests is the necessity for a level of benefits sufficient to induce workers to leave state firms (see also Micklewright and Nagy 1995 for a similar view). However, if benefits are too generous, the policy can backfire. Additional caution is warranted in that high benefits may have adverse effects on the incentives of the unemployed to search for jobs. In such a case, unemployment, while costly for the budget may exert only weak pressures on private sector wages and thereby discourage job creation. The model can take this into account by assuming a very strong effect of benefits on unemployment. This rules out the existence of a balanced budget policy with high benefits. The only possible outcome under a tight budget constraint is that, despite high benefits, workers would not leave state firms as long as unemployment benefits were lower than state sector wages. Indeed, the probability of employment in the private sector would be so low that it is more attractive to stay in state firms.

(4.) An output or employment subsidy to the private sector shifts the UK curve upward, reducing the region of initial conditions that lead to a failed restructuring (Chadha and Coricelli

1995). Unemployment increases initially, however, worsening the budget balance. Analogous results are produced by subsidies to holding capital in the private sector.

(5.) Public investment can be considered as a way to increase initial K, improving chances for successful restructuring without increasing unemployment. This applies to investment in infrastructure or any other investment that increases the return on investment in the private sector. For this reason, the sharp contraction in public investment observed in most economies in transition appears particularly troublesome due to its adverse long-run effects.

(6.) The social services provided by firms can be easily treated in the analytical model discussed above by adding them to the wage paid to workers in the state sector. Assuming the benefits are paid as a lump sum, two cases can be distinguished. In one case, firms provide social benefits and pay benefits for each worker. This is equivalent to social security contributions. The second case is that in which the government provides these social services. If budget expenditures are fully funded by social security contributions, the two cases are equivalent. By contrast, if the government finances these expenditures through a deficit, then the second case is equivalent to a reduction in the tax burden on state firms. Of course, from the individual worker's point of view, benefits increase the actual remuneration for the employees in state firms, discouraging their exit from those firms.

In the context of hard budget constraints, the provision of services by enterprises does not have a significant effect on wage or employment decisions of state firms. In fact, rather than favoring labor hoarding, by increasing the financial burden on state firms, social services tend to have an adverse effect on state sector employment. This may explain the rapidity with which state firms have reduced social services typically provided by local governments in market economies. In cases where fringe benefits have increased, as in Hungary, the main cause seems to be the favorable tax treatment of fringe benefits relative to wage payments (Fajit and Lakatos 1993).

5. Empirical Evidence on the Dynamics of Output, Unemployment, and the Speed of Reform

Despite its simplicity, the model yields a few striking results:

Figure 3.9

Unemployment and Output

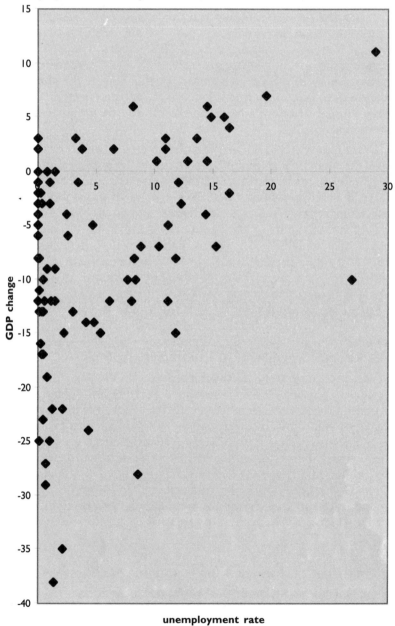

(1.) Unemployment and output are related by a highly non-linear function. In fact, during the first stages of reforms, unemployment increases together with output growth (figure 3.9).

(2.) The growth of the private sector is associated with higher unemployment.

(3.) Private sector growth negatively affects output growth, but only for a short initial period. The effects of private sector growth on output growth turns positive well before it leads to a downturn in unemployment.

(4.) The initial condition of the capital stock usable in productive sectors is crucial for the success of restructuring.

Table 3.2

Unemployment and Output Change (1989–94)

Dependent variable: Unemployment rate
All countries except countries in war
OLS regression

Variable	Coefficient	t-statistics
Constant	7.79	9.42
GDP change	0.47	3.70
GDP change squared	-0.01	-1.88
R-Squared	0.19	

Although a robust test of the theory is not feasible, we try to evaluate below whether these four predictions find some empirical support. We consider the eighteen reforming countries that form the entire sample of Eastern European economies, excepting countries involved in wars, for 1990–4.

Let us first consider the relationship between unemployment and output growth. A simple regression shows that output growth is positively correlated to the unemployment rate. In the above model this would imply that the sample is already in the segment of the bell-shaped curve that comes after the initial negative relationship (unemployment starts rising when the economy is in

Table 3.3a

Private Sector Development and Output Change

OLS regression, all countries 1989–1994

(i) Low level of development of private sector

Variable	Coefficient	t-statistics
Constant	-4.80	-2.60
Private sector	-17.08	-2.39

(ii) High level of development of private sector

Variable	Coefficient	t-statistics
Constant	-35.85	-3.33
Private sector	44.26	2.93

Table 3.3b

Private Sector Development and Unemployment

Variable	Coefficient	t-statistics
Constant	19.44	2.66
Private sector	78.79	3.45
Private sector squared	-22.23	-2.74

recession). However, if we add the square of output changes, it turns out that the data confirm the presence of a bell-shaped relationship between unemployment and growth (table 3.2).

Similarly, the impact of private sector growth on output growth turns out to be nonlinear in the sample. Indeed, if we split the sample between low private sector growth and high private sector growth and run two separate regressions, we obtain that at low private sector growth, output declines as the private sector grows (table 3.3a). However, at high levels of private sector development, output increases with private sector growth.[8]

Combining these results on unemployment and growth and on private sector development and growth, we can derive the impact of private sector growth on unemployment. Interestingly, the bell-shaped relationship predicted by the model seems to be supported by the data (table 3.3b). A panel regression linking unemployment to the index of private sector development and its square shows a positive significant coefficient on the level of private sector development, and a significantly negative coefficient on the square of the index. Thus, the relationship is nonlinear and describes a hump-shaped curve.

Finally, we analyzed the role of initial conditions. As noted in chapter 1, prereform liberalization seems to have played a crucial role in determining the success of reforms. We can consider the result to be indirect support for the findings of the model. Indeed, we can interpret the overall index of liberalization as a proxy of the quality of the initial capital stock, both physical and human.

5.1 Empirical Evidence on Fiscal Constraints and Feedback[9]

With the notable exception of the Czech Republic, reforms in Central and Eastern European economies (CEEs from now on) have been invariably associated with worsening fiscal balances. In view of the large fall in output that took place across the region, such a deterioration is not surprising. However, there seems to be a very weak correlation between output behavior and the budget; more structural sources seem to be at work. The pace of restructuring and unemployment and the relative dynamics of state and private firms, likely had an impact on the budget somehow independently of the behavior of aggregate output. Moreover, the sharp increase in unemployment and falling real wages have put pressure on social expenditures. Social expenditures, traditionally high in the previous regime of universal social protection, even increased in some cases. The relationship between budgetary developments and the characteristics and speed of restructuring reduce the informational role of the budget. Indeed, budget deficits may result from a strong commitment to fast and far-reaching market reforms rather than from a populist attitude, or from the maintenance of the status quo via large subsidies (Kornai 1993; Tanzi 1993).

Adopting the classification suggested by the EBRD and the World Bank (see chapter 1), we group CEEs into "fast" and "slow" reformers. This classification proves useful in identifying some key differences in fiscal developments and in fiscal policies. Consistent with our analytical model, we find that fiscal pressures become stronger while the transition progresses, and that they are more acute in the fast reforming countries. Thus, demands on governments to slow down restructuring mount, as do demands for compensating transfers to groups affected by reforms.

Governments face an important trade-off. Excessively tight budget constraints may yield perverse effects, as they may slow down restructuring. Indeed, a fast decline of state enterprises would lead to adverse fiscal effects by increasing unemployment expenditures and simultaneously reducing the tax base. These effects are particularly strong when the taxation is concentrated on state firms, while private firms largely escape taxation. Together with pressures arising from increasing income inequality and lobbying from specific interest groups, such as pensioners, fiscal constraints likely played a major role in the reform cycle observed in many CEEs, especially in determining the asymmetry between economic and political cycles. Examples of change over time in the speed of reforms are evident in the continuing delay of privatization. More generally, the widespread electoral successes of parties originating from former communist organizations testify to the pressures for changing the pace of reforms.

The next section reviews the nature of the fiscal crisis in CEEs, illustrating the weak link between aggregate output behavior and budget deficits. It also highlights some facts regarding the different behaviors of revenues and expenditures in fast and slow reformers. The key difference seems to relate to the combination of higher reduction in subsidies cum higher social expenditures in fast reforming countries. Such increase in expenditures appears to be the main cause of fiscal pressures, while the feared revenue collapse did not materialize. Section 5.3 discusses the main policy implications on the basis of the analytical model of section 4.

5.2 The Nature of the Fiscal Crisis

The economic transformation in Central and Eastern Europe has been associated with a deterioration of fiscal accounts (figure 3.10). Interestingly, the deterioration did not occur during the first year of reforms, despite the fact that the output decline was generally steeper at the outset of reforms. Given that reforms have been generally associated with a jump in the rate of inflation, there is no correlation between budget deficits and high inflation. In fact, in some instances (Poland and former Czechoslovakia), high inflation coincided with budget surpluses, suggesting the presence of a "reverse Tanzi effect." In both coun-

Figure 3.10

Budget Deficits in Central and Eastern Europe, 1989–95

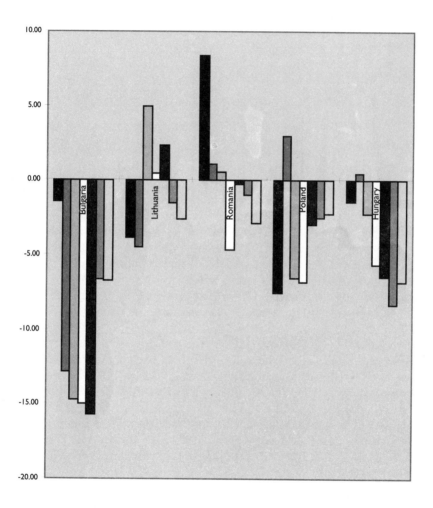

Table 3.4

Correlation Matrix: 6 Countries, 1989–93

	Budget balance	GDP growth	Unemployment rate
Budget balance	I		
GDP growth	-0.1 I	I	
Unemployment rate	0.54	-0.04	I

Source: EBRD, *Transition Report*, October 1994

tries, such an outcome was mostly due to the taxation of paper profits determined by the fact that inflation boosted the nominal value of inventories. In Poland, for example, profit taxes jumped from 8.5 percent in 1989 to 15.2 percent of GDP in 1990, and then declined to an average of 4 percent during the period 1991-3 (IMF 1994; Schaffer 1995). Therefore, factors other than short-term aggregate output behavior likely affected the behavior of the budget deficit. In particular, it can be conjectured that the dynamics of the budget are related to the pace of economic restructuring, summarized by the asymmetric dynamics of declining state firms and growing private sectors.

5.2.1 Interpreting Budget Deficits

Isolating evidence of the relationship between budgets and the pace of restructuring is not an easy task. Indeed, how the speed of transition is defined is not independent from fiscal variables. For instance, one can define the speed of restructuring in relation to the speed at which subsidies to state enterprises are dismantled. Notwithstanding methodological difficulties, there are several stylized facts indicating the dependence of fiscal accounts on the pace of reforms.

Table 3.4 shows that the behavior of budget deficits during the period 1989-93 is significantly correlated with the evolution of the unemployment rate, rather than with output. Indeed, the correlation with the behavior of GDP is very weak, although of the expected negative sign. The correlation matrix also shows that changes in GDP are weakly associated with movements in the rate of unemployment. The data cover six CEEs (Bulgaria, Czech Republic, Hungary, Poland, Romania, and Slovakia) over the period

Table 3.5

Budget Deficits, GDP Growth, and Unemployment Rate, 1989–93

OLS regression, Observations: 35
Dependent variable: Budget balance as a percentage of GDP
t-statistics in parentheses

B/GDP =	0.43	-0.06 y	+ 0.42 UR
	(0.39)	(-0.56)	(3.60)*
$R^2 = 0.29$			

* significant at the 1 percent level

B = Budget deficit

y = Rate of growth of real GDP

UR = Rate of unemployment

1989–93. Using the same data, table 3.5 reports the results of a simple regression that includes simultaneously changes in GDP and the rate of unemployment as explanatory variables of the budget balance (measured in terms of GDP). The coefficient for the rate of unemployment is statistically significant and quite high, while the coefficient for the change in GDP is not statistically significant.

These facts suggest first that the fiscal implications of unemployment go beyond the simple relationship between the budget and short-term movements in GDP, and second, that fiscal pressure is likely to continue even during the phase of recovery in transition economies, one reason being the asymmetric dynamics of output and unemployment. The role of unemployment, as we have argued, can be considered a summary indicator of the role of restructuring in the economy. In particular, according to the model developed in section 4, discrepancies between unemployment and GDP behavior may signal the presence of restructuring in the economy.

As shown in table 3.1, using the EBRD classification of countries on the basis of the speed of reform, fast reformers display a significantly higher ratio of unemployment rates to GDP growth.[10] This can be interpreted as an indication of the positive correlation between unemployment and structural change during the transition. However, the Czech Republic's presence in the fast

Table 3.6

International Comparison of Government Accounts

	Arithmetic mean for Western economies	Standard deviation	Hungary 1989	Hungary 1992	Poland 1989	Poland 1992
Total Revenue	48.5	8.4	61.2	57.7	33.8	39.5
Tax revenue	41.1	6.4	50.5	42.7	30.3	31.6
Income taxes	13.9	5.7	13.7	10.5	8.5	10.2
Individual	9.7	5.6	5.5	7.9	0.0	4.2
Enterprises	4.2	5.0	8.2	2.6	8.5	6.0
Social security contr.	10.9	5.5	15.9	14.1	8.7	10.0
Payroll taxes	0.4	0.6	0.0	0.0		
Property taxes	2.4	3.3	0.4	0.0		
Domestic taxes on goods and services	12.0	2.4	17.6	12.8	10.4	10.2
VAT 1/	6.0	2.3	7.9	6.3		
Excises 1/	3.5	1.1	5.6	5.9		
Other 2/	2.5	2.5	4.1	0.6	10.4	10.2
Taxes on international trade	0.5	0.8	2.9	3.6	0.0	2.0
Other taxes	1.6	2.8	0.1	1.7	2.8	
Nontax revenues	6.5	2.7	10.3	15.1	3.5	7.9
Capital revenues	0.6	0.3	0.4	0.0		
	Arithmetic mean for Western economies	Standard deviation	Hungary 1989	Hungary 1992	Poland 1989	Poland 1992
Total expenditure and lending repayments	49.8	6.7	63.6	63.4		
Total expenditure	49.7	6.5	63.6	63.4	33.8	50.3
Current expenditure	45.6	7.2	56.4	55.3	36.5	47.3
Expenditure on goods and services	19.4	3.9	22.1	18.3	7.9	13.7
Wages and salaries	12.0	2.8	8.3	8.9	4.2	7.6
Other goods and services	7.4	2.1	13.6	9.4	3.7	6.1
Interest payments	4.8	2.1	3.2	6.1	1.0	3.0
Subsidies & current transfers	21.5	5.4	31.1	30.0	21.7	26.3
Subsidies	2.0	1.4	15.5	5.8	9.1	4.4
Transfers to households and non-profit inst.	16.2	5.2	15.6	24.2	12.6	21.9
Capital expenditures	4.0	1.1	7.2	8.1	3.4	3.0
Capital transfers	1.0	0.5	1.9	1.8	n.a.	n.a.
Lending minus repayments	0.2	0.9	0.1	0	n.a.	n.a.

122

reformers group represents an important exception; a summary measure of speed of reforms may be misleading. In particular, the speed of privatization appears largely independent of the speed of reforms in other areas, especially macroeconomic.

One factor seems to be that high unemployment conflicts with speed of privatization. In the country in which privatization has proceeded fastest, the Czech Republic, the unemployment rate has been the lowest. Moreover, the comparative experiences of the Czech and Slovak Republics clearly illustrate the negative relationship between unemployment and speed of privatization. After the split at the end of 1992 both countries had the same privatization policies. However, pressures to slow down privatization mounted in Slovakia, and by the end of 1994 the Slovak government adopted an explicit shift in privatization strategy, implying a slowdown. If one compares the main economic indicators of the two republics, the sharply higher unemployment rate in the Slovak Republic stands out as the most important difference. While there could be several channels through which unemployment and speed of privatization interact, the fiscal channel we focus on here is likely to be an important one. The next section analyzes the behavior of revenues and expenditure behind the movements of the budget balance.

5.2.2 Revenues and Expenditures

Before discussing the behavior of revenues and expenditures in the two groups of countries, it may be useful to briefly evaluate the "size" of the government and the structure of taxes and expenditures in CEEs on the basis of indicators from market economies. We focus on the former Czechoslovakia, Hungary, and Poland, and contrast their data with those of Western Europe.

5.2.3 "Size" of the Government and Structure of Revenues and Expenditures

If compared to a sample of Western European countries, the share of income intermediated by the state in Bulgaria, the former Czechoslovakia, Hungary, Poland, and Romania before the start of reforms was high (table 3.6).[11] Among the CEEs, Poland and Romania displayed significantly smaller-sized governments. Table 3.7 shows that, over time, the size of the government declined sharply in the Czech Republic, Slovak Republic, Bulgaria, and Romania, but not in Hungary and Poland.

Table 3.7

Government Expenditures (in percent of GDP)

	1989	1993	change
Bulgaria			
Social security benefits	10.4	15.8	5.4
Subsidies	15.5	4.8	-10.7
Cap. expenditures	5.5	1.9	-3.6
Total expenditures	61.5	51.2	-10.3
Czech Republic			
Social security benefits	13.6	13.5	-0.1
Subsidies	25	4.4	-20.6
Cap. expenditures	8.5	4.2	-4.3
Total expenditures	72.3	47.5	-24.8
Slovak Republic			
Social security benefits	13.6	16.7	3.1
Subsidies	25	4.8	-20.2
Cap. expenditures	8.5	5.3	-3.2
Total exp	72.3	55.1	-17.2
Hungary			
Social security benefits	14.4	18.2	3.8
Subsidies	12.1	4.8	-7.3
Cap. expenditures	6.6	6.2	-0.4
Total expenditures	61	60.5	-0.5
Poland			
Social security benefits	11.2	20.4	9.2
Subsidies	12.9	3	-9.9
Cap. expenditures	3.3	1.5	-1.8
Total expenditures	48.9	48.4	-0.5
Romania			
Social security benefits	9.5	8.9	-0.6
Subsidies	5.7	5.5	-0.2
Cap. expenditures	17.6	4.3	-13.3
Total expenditures	42.6	31	-11.6

Source: IMF (1994b)

Before reforms, a central role for enterprises characterized the fiscal flows in CEEs. Payroll taxes and profit taxes had the lion's share of total revenues. On the expenditure side, producer subsidies were very significant; social security benefits were also high, while capital expenditures varied significantly across countries, with Romania as the only case exhibiting a very high share of capital expenditures in total expenditures (41 percent in

1989). In contrast to popular views, there is little evidence that actual expenditures were significantly underestimated due to the important role of state enterprises in providing social services and other fringe benefits to employees. Measured flows of these benefits indicate that their magnitude was about 3 to 5 percent of total labor costs. Given the relatively low share of wages in GDP in CEEs, the weight of benefits provided by enterprises can be estimated at about 1 to 2 percent of GDP (Fajith and Lakatos 1994; Earle 1994). This, in turn, implies that budget data on social expenditures do not significantly underestimate actual social expenditures in Central and Eastern Europe. By contrast, studies of Russia point to much larger benefits provided by enterprises (Commander and Jackman 1994).

However, the low figures for social benefits provided directly by firms in CEEs may be misleading. Indeed, the prices used to evaluate the benefits may be very low, as they are based on operational costs and do not take into account the implicit subsidies obtained by using facilities owned by the firms. A proper accounting, for instance, of rental costs for facilities used is likely to raise significantly the value of the benefits provided by firms. Therefore, the fiscal impact of transferring to the state the provision of benefits provided by many enterprises may be somewhat relevant (Earle 1994).

The divestiture of social benefits provided by enterprises is also affected by the process of reallocation of resources from state to private enterprises. Interestingly, survey data for Poland suggest that newly created private enterprises do not provide any benefits. However, corporatized or privatized enterprises tend to provide levels of benefits similar to those of state-owned enterprises (Estrin, Schaffer, and Singh 1994).

Overall, before reforms CEEs were characterized by high expenditures on subsidies and current transfers. After reforms a major redistribution occurred from subsidies to transfers. As a result, the sum of these two expenditures in terms of GDP was stable in Hungary, while it increased in Poland. Only in the former Czechoslovakia was there a significant decline. In relation to Western Europe, Hungary and Poland spend a smaller proportion of GDP in goods and services and wage and salaries. Hungary maintained relatively high expenditures in public investment. By contrast, Poland displayed a sharp fall, which brought the ratio of public investment to GDP below the average levels of Western

Table 3.8

Government Revenues (in percent of GDP)

	1989	1993	change
Bulgaria			
Profit tax	23.2	5.6	-17.6
Wage tax	4.1	5.2	1.1
Social security	9.6	9.0	-0.6
Total revenue	59.8	37.4	-22.4
Czech Republic			
Profit tax	11.0	7.5	-3.5
Wage tax	6.9	3.3	-3.6
Social security	15.0	16.0	1.0
Total revenue	69.5	48.5	-21.0
Slovak Republic			
Profit tax	11.0	6.5	-4.5
Wage tax	6.9	4.3	-2.6
Social security	15.0	12.6	-2.4
Total revenue	69.5	48.1	-21.4
Hungary			
Profit tax	8.1	2.2	-5.9
Wage tax	5.5	8.4	2.9
Social security	14.3	14.3	0.0
Total revenue	59.6	54.1	-5.5
Poland			
Profit tax	9.7	5.3	-4.4
Wage tax	3.4	9.1	5.7
Social security	7.4	9.9	2.5
Total revenue	41.4	45.5	4.1
Romania			
Profit tax	7.3	3.5	-3.8
Wage tax	6.3	6.6	0.3
Social security	6.7	8.5	1.8
Total revenue	51.0	30.8	-20.2

Source: IMF (1994b)

Europe. In general, these three CEEs spend much less than Western Europe on labor market programs, both active and passive, taking into account the high rates of unemployment (Scarpetta, Boeri, and Reutersward 1994).

Finally, capital expenditures fell sharply in Romania, Bulgaria, and Poland, while they slightly increased in the former Czechoslovakia and Hungary (table 3.8, above). The compression of public investments in the first three countries was so large that their capital expenditures fell below those in Western European countries. For countries characterized by poor infrastructure, such a development should be a cause for concern, as it may deter the growth of the private sector.

As to the structure of revenues, the comparison of Hungary and Poland with Western Europe suggests four observations (table 3.8): (1.) Hungary had a structure of revenues similar to that of Western Europe even before 1990, and it further converged to it after 1990; (2.) in Poland and the former Czechoslovakia, the share of enterprise taxes in total revenues was much higher than in Western economies; (3.) after reforms, Poland shows a convergence to the structure of Western economies, with a shift from enterprise to household taxation; (4.) a similar process started in the Czech Republic in 1993; nevertheless revenues from enterprises remain higher than in Western economies.

Thus, the so-called McKinnon problem (McKinnon 1991), linked to the heavy reliance on revenues from state enterprises was rapidly overcome in the three more advanced CEEs. Moreover, while revenues from profit taxes declined, social security contributions increased. Overall, in the three advanced CEEs, there was no collapse in revenues even from state enterprises. The contribution of private firms to tax revenues remains low compared with their share in output (even neglecting the underground economy). A general feature of reform has been the increase in the importance of foreign trade taxes. Because of the very low starting level, the share of these taxes remains low, especially if compared with developing countries (EBRD 1994).

VAT was introduced in July 1993 in Poland, in January 1993 in both the Czech and the Slovak Republics, and in October 1993 in Bulgaria, while in Hungary it was introduced as early as 1988 together with the introduction of the personal income tax. In Poland, for instance, during 1993, the year of its introduction, revenues from VAT exceeded those for the old turnover taxes.

5.2.4 Behind the Crisis: The Behavior of Revenues and Expenditures

Initial expectations viewed the risk of a fiscal crisis largely dependent on the likely collapse of tax revenues associated with a shrinking state-enterprise sector, the traditional tax base (McKinnon 1991). In contrast with these expectations, the main

Table 3.9

**Changes in Government Expenditures, 1989–93
(in percent of GDP)**

Slow reformers without Russia

Social security benefits	2.40
Subsidies	-5.45
Cap. expenditures	-8.45
Total expenditures	-10.95

Fast reformers

Social security benefits	4.00
Subsidies	-14.50
Cap. expenditures	-2.42
Total expenditures	-10.75

Source: IMF (1994b)

pressures on the budget came from growing social expenditures (Barbone and Marchetti 1994). Among those, the largest weight has fallen on pension expenditures, leading some observers to talk of a "pensioners' power" threatening the reform process (Sachs 1995).

5.2.4.1 Expenditures

Using the distinction between fast and slow reforming countries, it is evident that social security expenditures increased more in fast than in slow reformers (table 3.9). Moreover, subsidies fell much more in the fast reformer group. In contrast, total expenditures fell on average by the same proportion in the two groups. Thus, while fast reformers have absorbed the impact of the subsidy cuts in higher social security expenditures, slow reformers have opted for maintaining higher subsidies that, in the short run, may have moderated social expenditures. An alternative interpretation is that, given an overall budget constraint, slow reformers had less room for social expenditures. This by itself may have contributed to a slowdown in restructuring, because of the unattractively low income from being unemployed or out of the labor force.

Within social expenditures, the evidence is that the main pressures on public expenditure arose from pensions and other social benefits, rather than from unemployment benefits. However, the main source of increased pension expenditure has generally been the increase in the number of pensioners leaving employment before the legal retirement age.[12] Thus, the increase in expenditure for pensions reflected largely the adjustment in the labor market. Expenditures for social benefits were also largely determined by transfers to unemployed that exhausted their entitlement to unemployment benefits. One possible interpretation is that the electoral power of pensioners allows them to protect their perceived interests.[13] Another, possibly complementary, interpretation links pension expenditure to the overall transition process and, in particular, to labor market dynamics.

By their nature, pensions raise important intertemporal issues. Recognizing that transition implies a temporary fall in real incomes, equity considerations call for an income transfer to people who will not benefit from the future fruits of the transition. Pensioners, and the older generations in general, are a case in point. It may be possible to find substitutability for older workers between wage demands and pensions. Social benefits therefore should be assessed in a general framework that takes into account the effects of benefits on wages and their general support for reforms. Moreover, as noted above, an important determinant of the increase in pensions was the increase in the number of pensioners due to the labor shedding that initially took the form of early retirement. These expenditures are thus seen as a by-product of employment restructuring. It is worth noting that the increased number of pensioners implied that real pensions per capita actually declined. Real pensions declined significantly in Hungary and the former Czechoslovakia, and, much less, in Poland. The average pension is indeed low in these countries, often not even ensuring a level of income above the poverty line, thus failing to achieve one very important objective of state-run pension systems (World Bank 1994a).

It is probable that the main reason for using pensions as the central social stabilizer to redistribute income in favor of groups adversely affected by reforms has been institutional inertia, which led to the maintenance of some features of the old system of universal social protection. The financial viability of pension schemes in countries such as Hungary and Poland is dubious. For instance,

Table 3.10

**Change in Government Revenues, 1989–83
(in percent of GDP)**

Slow reformers without Russia

Profit tax	-10.70
Wage tax	0.70
Social security	0.60
Total revenue	-21.30

Fast reformers

Profit tax	-4.57
Wage tax	0.60
Social security	0.27
Total revenue	-10.95

Source: Author's calculation on data from IMF (1994b)

social security contributions to be paid by enterprises are project-ed (in an unchanged pension system) to grow in Hungary from 34 percent in 1994 to about 38 percent by the year 2019 (World Bank 1994b). This high burden tends to push workers into the informal sector, reducing the tax base and generating a vicious cir-cle that puts a higher burden on the formal sector.

Despite the fall in unit labor costs between 1989 and 1992, social security contributions increased in relation to GDP in both Poland and Hungary. The level in Hungary is comparable to those in northern European countries, traditionally characterized by a very high wedge between wages and labor costs. Maintenance of these levels is also likely to be an incentive for the flourishing of an underground economy, which for countries with very high debt-to-GDP ratios may prove a serious problem in the medium run. The high rates of social security contributions probably bol-stered the mushrooming second economy in these countries. Thus, the fiscal channel may also help to explain the apparently puzzling phenomenon of fast-growing new private sectors in countries where privatization policies have been relatively slow (for example, Poland and Hungary).

Table 3.11

**Effect of Discretionary Policy Changes on Revenues/GDP Ratios
(in percent of GDP)**

	Corporate taxes	Payroll taxes	Indirect taxes	Incomes taxes	Foreign trade taxes	All policy changes changes	Total tax revenue change
Bulgaria (1990–93)	2.5	2.8	0.2	1.7	1.5	8.7	-18.4
Czechoslovakia (1990–92)	-8.3	0.3	0.2	-3.3	-0.8	-11.8	-17.3
Czech Republic (1993)	-2.6	4.0	-3.9	1.0	-0.2	-1.7	1.7
Slovak Republic (1993)	-2.1	4.3	-4.0	1.4	—	-0.4	-4.7
Hungary (1989–93)	-2.2	4.3	1.3	0.8	-2.5	1.7	-7.1
Poland (1989–93)	0.8	2.1	2.7	2.7	3.1	11.4	-1.0
Romania (1990–93)	-2.5	6.5	3.1	-9.4	-0.9	-3.2	-17.0

Source: International Monetary Fund, (1994)

5.2.4.2 Revenues

In 1993 the distribution of revenues in different tax and nontax sources was similar in the two groups of countries (that is, fast and slow reformers). However, clear differences emerge if one looks at the changes in various tax items that took place after reforms (table 3.10). For the period 1989–93, a collapse of profit tax revenues is noticeable in the slow reformer group, a collapse that did not occur in the fast reformer group. Thus, pressure on the tax-paying firms, mainly state enterprises, has been much higher in the fast reformer group. Furthermore, if one combines the tax pressure with the larger contraction in subsidies, it is apparent that the overall pressure has been far stronger in fast reforming countries. This higher pressure may be considered as a key distinguishing characteristic of the faster speed of reform.

It is important to note, however, that even within the group of fast reformers there were significant differences. Indeed, the Czech Republic (and Slovakia) has shown a different pattern of revenue behavior, that in turn is linked to a different pattern of expenditure behavior. As noted above, both expenditures and revenues have declined after reforms, albeit from very high levels. The fall in subsidies has been accompanied by a fall in tax rev-

131

enue. In the Czech Republic there was no explosion of social expenditure, so the cut in subsidies could be translated into a fall in the tax burden. This has been largely due to discretionary policy changes, implemented especially in the first two years of transition, when the Czech and Slovak Republics were still part of Czechoslovakia.[14] Table 3.11 indicates that about 70 percent of the decline in tax revenue in the former CSFR during 1990-2 can be attributed to policy changes. By contrast, in Hungary and Poland, policy changes were aimed at increasing tax pressure on the economy.

Taxation of the private sector has been elusive. In Poland, for which data are available for the recorded private sector, the contribution of the private sector to tax revenues was much smaller than its contribution to output. In 1993, for instance, the private sector accounted for 24 percent of the sum of profit, dividend, and excess wage tax, while its share in total sales was 48 percent. In industry, the private-sector share in the same set of taxes was 12 percent, while its share in total sales was 32 percent.[15]

An important phenomenon that affected several transition economies has been the growth of tax arrears, or deferred (often indefinitely) payments. This phenomenon has reached a significant size, estimated in flow terms at around 2 to 3 percent of GDP in countries such as Hungary, Poland, and the Slovak Republic. Microeconomic data show that these arrears were concentrated in state firms that were having financial difficulties. Thus, tax arrears can be interpreted as a form of subsidy to these firms. In this perspective, tax arrears might have been the channel through which state firms in difficulties have postponed closure or downsizing. The fact that these arrears have developed particularly in recent years tends to confirm the view that fiscal pressure was loosened, slowing down the pace of restructuring in countries with high unemployment rates and attendant high social expenditures. Indeed, tax arrears grew more in countries in which tax pressure, as net of subsidies, was stronger (Hungary and Poland). The interesting finding is that firms accounting for the largest tax arrears did not fall into arrears in payments to other enterprises or banks (Schaffer 1995). This suggests that firms counted on the fact that the government would not initiate bankruptcy proceedings against them, while firms or banks would have.

To sum up, fast reformers began the transition by putting strong pressure on state firms by drastically reducing subsidies and in most cases raising effective taxation. The relevant measure of fiscal pressure on state-owned firms is the taxation net of subsidies (Barbone and Marchetti 1994). As transition progressed and unemployment increased, there was pressure for slowing down transition in countries with high unemployment. The loosening of fiscal pressure came about through the tolerated growth of tax arrears and, in the case of Poland, the reduction of dividend tax and excess wage tax. Thus, the slowdown of the pace of restructuring was not only associated with the political cycle, but also with the perverse effects coming from tight fiscal constraints. This view is consistent with the analytical model put forward by Dewatripont and Roland (1992a; 1992b).

6. Concluding Remarks

This chapter focused on the role of fiscal constraints and policies in the process of transition. The specific characteristic of the transition process is that social costs tend to follow a nonlinear, hump-shaped path. Before enjoying the benefits of market reforms, several groups in society suffer severe losses. Whether this is due to an absolute fall in living standards or to a sudden increase in relative positions, and thus income inequality, is still an open question. Measurement of real output and hence of welfare changes is hardly possible in economies that moved from a shortage to a market economy. However, the sudden increase in unemployment, and its persistence, leave little doubt regarding the magnitude of the adverse shock to the economy. In this perspective, the widespread reversal of support to reformist governments—with the exception of the Czech Republic—may indeed have economic underpinnings.

We argued that an excessive concern with short-term fiscal positions may have in fact contributed to such reversal. Not only are fiscal indicators highly ambiguous during the transition, but budget tightening can determine perverse effects on the process of restructuring. Three main conclusions stand out. First, there is a close connection between the speed of reforms, cuts in subsidies and the related imposition of harder constraints, and the increase in social expenditures. Second, the increase in social expenditures was the primary force behind worsening budget deficits. Such an increase was ill conceived, as it was concentrated in pensions and carried the seeds of negative long-term consequences. Third, and relatedly, the need for initial transfers to "losers" to create support and, in fact, foster reforms should have been recognized, and appropriate schemes designed (on pension reform see Holzmann 1994). This has important implications for unemployment benefit policy, as well as for the design and reform of pension schemes.

4

Income Distribution and the Dynamics of Reform

1. Introduction

Earlier we showed that the fiscal implications of unemployment and the reallocation of labor from a declining state to a growing private sector can generate pressure to slow down restructuring, and thus to soften the constraints on state firms and even reverse the process of reducing subsidies to them. The main mechanism of labor reallocation worked through the fiscal impact of unemployment. Another channel can be identified in the social impact of unemployment. Indeed, the opposition to sustained fast reforms can grow together with the increase in unemployment. However, focusing only on unemployment may be misleading. Indeed, support for restructuring and fast reforms is likely to be affected as well by developments in real incomes in the population. As stressed in the development and growth literature, a large factor affecting political attitudes is the degree to which income distribution is unequal.

This chapter discusses this channel, using the same two-sector framework used earlier, that is, the model developed by Chadha and Coricelli (1994). That model, indeed, generates a Kuznets curve, which parallels the bell-shaped curve depicting the behavior of unemployment during the transition. The value added gained from analyzing the behavior of income distribution during transition is given by the possibility of a nonsynchronized behavior of income distribution, output growth, and unemployment. Specifically, inequality may continue to increase well beyond the turning point of output and unemployment. This may help to explain the apparent paradox of dissatisfaction with reformist governments in countries in which the economy was undergoing a significant recovery of output (for example, Poland).

More generally, the model permits an analysis of the behavior of income distribution in a system in which relative wages, employment in the two sectors, and unemployment are endogenous and vary over time. This seems to be a step forward in the literature, which usually is based on the exogeneity of several of these variables.

2. Empirical Evidence

The view of socialism as a regime in which income distribution was much more egalitarian than in market economies has been a cornerstone of the comparative analysis of socialist versus market economies (Atkinson and Micklewright 1992). This view has often been criticized by those who argued that, in fact, income inequalities were as large in socialist countries as in market economies. Knowledge of the income distribution starting point prior to reforms is crucial to assessing the extent of either inertia or change in the various countries. Analyzing four countries (Czechoslovakia, Hungary, Poland, and the fSU), Atkinson and Micklewright conclude that while income distribution in the prereform regimes (measured during the mid-1980s) was much more equal in Czechoslovakia and Hungary than in a market economy like that of the United Kingdom, the gap was much smaller between the USSR and the UK. Poland was somewhere between the extremes, although closer to the USSR than to Czechoslovakia. Table 4.1 displays the country ranking in terms of the Gini coefficient.

Thus, within an overall picture of lower income inequality in planned economies, there were very large differences across countries, with Czechoslovakia and Hungary standing out as rather egalitarian countries. Looking at the changes after the full-fledged reforms of the 1990s, it appears that the prereform ranking has been confirmed. The sharp increase in inequality in Hungary cannot be found in studies that looked at expenditure data rather than income data (Newbery 1994). Nevertheless, the data suggest three main observations. First, preferences for more equal income distribution continued to operate, especially in the Czech Republic, while, second, Poland and the USSR jumped to

Table 4.1

Gini Coefficients, Prereform and Postreform Periods

	1985	1993–94
Czechoslovakia*	19.9	20/27
Hungary†	20.9	28
Poland	25.3	31
USSR‡	25.6	36
UK	29.7	

* In 1993–94, 20 is for the Czech Republic and 27 for Slovakia.

† Instead of 1985, it is 1982 for Hungary.

‡ In 1993–94, it is only for Russia.

Source: Atkinson and Micklewright (1992), p. 112 and Milanovic (1996).

inequality indicators above those observed in the UK in the 1980s. Third, the low inequality indices for the Czech Republic suggest that low unemployment can be an effective instrument to reduce inequality.

The empirical work carried out especially at the World Bank highlights three additional features that prima facie support the findings of our analytical model (Milanovic 1996): (1.) Inequality increases with private sector growth during the initial stages of transition; (2.) inequality increases with unemployment; (3.) increased wage differentials are an important determinant of increasing inequality. With the exception of Romania, increasing wage differentials account for a large proportion—generally more than 50 percent—of the increase in the Gini coefficient (Milanovic 1996). Table 4.2 displays the change in the Gini coefficient from the prereform period to the postreform period. The magnitude of the increase in income inequality brought about by the movement towards a market economy is striking. An increase in inequality of such proportions, and achieved in such a short time interval, is probably unprecedented. Although the increase in inequality reflects the abandonment of the artificially compressed income distribution structure in the old regime, it is likely that during the transition there is an overshooting of inequality indicators that will prevail at the end of the transition period. Although

Table 4.2

Change in Income Inequality* 1987–88 versus 1993–4

	1987–88	1993–94
Czech Republic	19	19
Hungary	21	23
Poland	26	31
Slovak Republic	20	20
Bulgaria	23	34
Slovenia	24	28
Romania	23	29
All transition countries, including fSU	24	32

* Gini coefficient, based on income data

Source: Milanovic (1996)

poverty has reached extremely high levels even in such countries as Poland, considered the "success story" of transition, current levels of income inequality should improve over time. The importance of unemployment as a predictor for poverty in the case of Poland suggests that poverty should decline as unemployment begins to decline.

Country studies tend to emphasize the role of restructuring, unemployment, and private-sector growth as determinants of increasing inequality and poverty. Thus, increasing inequality may be the inevitable cost of successful transformation. However, cross-country data, and in particular the comparison between CEE countries and the countries of the fSU, point to an even larger increase in inequality in countries where reforms proceeded at a slower pace. Slowing down transition does not seem to reduce income inequality. Moreover, fSU countries display the highest Gini coefficients and the largest increase in the coefficient after reforms despite the absence of significant unemployment. Thus, prima facie, the argument we put forward on the basis of our theoretical model seems to conflict with the experience of the fSU. However, both the Gini coefficients and the unemployment data for the fSU should be regarded with caution. The nature of transition in most fSU countries differed from that prevailing in CEE countries. A key difference is due to the role of provider of social services that firms in the fSU, but not in Central and Eastern

Europe, continued to play. The provision of such benefits implies that recorded income severely understates the income received by workers. In several instances, such as in the case of significant wage arrears, social benefits represent the bulk of income received by workers. Moreover, benefits tend to be equally distributed. Thus, de facto, they flatten the income distribution curve. Lacking a proper measurement of the market value of these benefits, measured incomes give a misleading picture. The true income distribution should therefore be much more even than that revealed by incomes data. As part of expenditure is directed to these services, even expenditure data may suffer from the bias mentioned above.

The role of firms as provider of social services helps to explain the low level of unemployment registered in the fSU during the first years of transition. The combination of low unemployment benefits and high benefits associated with a job in the firm sharply reduced the scope for unemployment. Thus, despite the collapse in output, unemployment rates have remained extremely low and restructuring limited. In sum, a proper measurement of income flows, including social benefits, would likely reduce the indicators of income inequality. This would be consistent with the model that predicts that income inequality will increase with the increase of unemployment.

As the income of the unemployed tends to be much lower than that of the employed, increasing inequality implies that a large proportion of the population falls into low-income brackets. Indeed, increasing inequality coincided with increasing poverty. Table 4.3 reports a regression carried out by Milanovic (1996),

Table 4.3

Explaining the increase in poverty

Dependent variable: Change in poverty headcount, 1988 to 1993/4

Constant	ΔIncome	ΔGini	PPPIncome	ΔLib
13.5	-0.61	1.05	-0.005	2.5
1.4	6.5	2.5	2.7	0.2
R^2=0.86				

Source: Milanovic (1996)

which shows the strong correlation between the increase in poverty and the change in income inequality, summarized by the Gini coefficient.

This chapter focuses on a narrow aspect of the role of income inequality in the transition process. In particular, it develops a model that generates a Kuznets curve emerging during the transition process. The interesting feature of the model is the non-synchronized dynamic among output, unemployment, and income inequality. Indeed, the increase in inequality tends to persist well beyond the turning point for both output and unemployment. This may provide some insight into the peculiar dynamics of political support—or lack of it—in reforming countries. Opposition to reformist governments has grown even in countries in which overall economic activity, such as aggregate GDP, was showing clear signs of recovery (in Poland, for instance). Thus, the model offers an economic explanation for a political phenomenon that tends to be explained in terms either of the inability of people to understand economic reality (gap between reality and perception), or in terms of pressure groups—say, pensioners and workers in state-owned companies—trying to slow down the process of reform. The model seems to fit the observed tendency of opponents to reformist governments, not favoring stopping the reform process itself, but rather favoring rendering such reforms more "socially acceptable."

3. A Simple Framework

Consider the model discussed in chapter 3 for the case in which growth of the private sector is driven by exogenous factors (technological change or accumulation of human capital). The effects of the sectoral reallocation of labor on income distribution can be analyzed by measuring the evolution over time of the Gini coefficient. When the process of labor reallocation starts, income is fairly equally distributed among the population. The proportion of people employed in the state sector is very large, while the unemployment rate is low. At the end of the reallocation process income is again equally distributed. The economy is only composed of private sector workers and there is no unemployment.

The key issue is to analyze the change in income distribution during the transition. Two main forces affect such evolution over time. First, the sectoral composition of employment changes:

140

Figure 4.1

Unemployment and Income Distribution

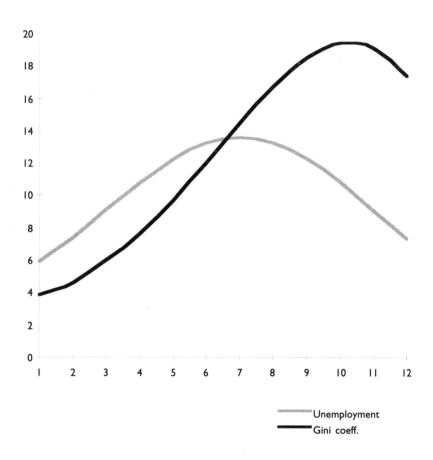

employment in the state sector shrinks continuously while employment in the private sector expands continuously. Second, the ratio between private sector and state sector wages follows a nonlinear pattern. As employment in the state sector declines, wages rise because the marginal product of labor in the state sector rises. The behavior of wages in the private sector mirrors the path of unemployment, as private sector wages are a decreasing function of the unemployment rate. In the early stages of the reallocation process, as unemployment increases, wages fall. After unemployment peaks, wages in the private sector begin to rise.

Inequality in income distribution reflects both the changes in the sectoral composition of employment and changes in relative wages. In the early stages of development the inequality unambiguously widens for two reasons. First, unemployment grows as an increasing share of the labor force is laid off from the state sector. The unemployed receive unemployment benefits that are always lower than state sector wages. Simultaneously, the private sector expands. In the early phases of restructuring, private sector wages are higher than those in the state sector. These two mechanisms tend to increase inequality in income distribution.

The dynamics of the restructuring process imply that inequality must narrow after a critical stage. Again, there are two main channels at work. The first is related to the dynamics of the reallocation of labor across sectors. Private employment monotonically increases, state employment monotonically decreases. An increasing share of workers are employed in the same sector getting the same wage. Unemployment is also declining, so there is a declining number of people who get unemployment benefits. The second is due to the evolution of wages. While the state-sector wage is always increasing along the development path, the private-sector wage follows a U-pattern. Thus, over time the gap between private- and state-sector wages narrows. This dampens the effects of income inequality associated with the shift of workers from the state sector to the private sector.

Figure 4.1 puts together all the elements and illustrates the evolution over time of income inequality, measured by the Gini coefficient. It is apparent that the path of income inequality describes a Kuznets curve. The important finding of the model is that income inequality tends to increase even after unemployment has reached its peak. The asymmetry between the two curves during transition points to the limits of unemployment as a measure of underlying pressures on governments (see Rodrik 1995 for a similar point).

4. Pressures for Policy Reversal

Przeworski (1991) identified unemployment as a main source of political difficulties during the transition. His political model assumes an underlying pattern of unemployment and output very similar to the one produced by our model. The nonlinear path of output and unemployment, in Przeworski, determines the dynamics of political support. In his analysis, radical reforms are characterized by a larger initial fall in output and increase in unemployment, but a faster recovery than a gradual program. Both gradual and radical programs imply short-term costs with respect to a no-reform strategy. Przeworski reaches three main conclusions relevant to our analysis. (1.) If people preferred a gradual program, but a big-bang (or radical) program was nevertheless implemented, people will pressure (vote) for a slowdown of reforms as they experience the transitional costs of reforms. However, reforms will not be abandoned. (2.) If initial costs are very large, people who supported either gradual or radical reforms may vote for abandoning reforms. This event is more likely if reforms were gradual at the beginning, as the cost of undoing reforms will be smaller than in the case of a radical reform. (3.) There is a threshold point in time after which reforms will not be reversed. The closer such a threshold occurs to the starting point, the sooner will output recover. The point of no reversal is reached sooner with a radical reform package.

All three observations—which were made before the unfolding of political reversal in most of Central and Eastern Europe—capture some aspects of the postreform political dynamics in transitional economies. However, the analysis leaves unexplained the puzzling result of fading support for reforms in countries well beyond the turning point of output recovery. The asynchronized dynamics of output, unemployment, and income distribution may offer an explanation for such a puzzle. Of course, the relationship between income inequality and political support for reforms is complex. One extreme view is that income distribution does not matter in democracy, because the observed income distribution always reflects the preferences of at least the majority of the population. A similar, though less extreme view is that increasing inequality is inevitable during the shift from central planning to a market economy and that tolerance for inequality increases during the transition to a market economy. The latter is a manifestation of the Hirschman's "tunnel effect," according to which people will not be unhappy if other people get richer, as they see in the success of other people the signal of their own future success. However, it is hard to reach any general conclusion. Our analysis simply suggests that income inequality may represent an obstacle to sustaining reforms. We do not discuss welfare implications or the optimal path of income distribution. Nevertheless, the model implies a clear trade-off between income inequality and restructuring of the economy.

5. Policy Analysis

As to policy implications, the main results are that a reduction of the tax burden on state firms—or an increase in subsidies—tends to reduce inequality in the short run, at the cost of a slower restructuring. Figure 4.2 illustrates the relationship between speed of restructuring and income inequality. A larger pressure on

Figure 4.3

Unemployment and Speed of Reform

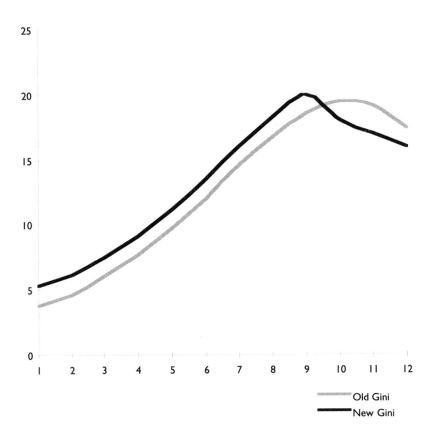

Old Gini
New Gini

state firms via higher taxation increases the speed of restructuring. This implies higher unemployment. Inequality increases initially, although it declines faster in the medium run.

As discussed earlier, changes in unemployment benefits have ambiguous effects. In particular, higher unemployment benefits may either increase or reduce inequality, depending on parameter values. The results on tax/subsidies on state firms provide a rationale for policy reversals (similar conclusions are reached by Rodrik (1995) in a model with exogenous labor dynamics). Reducing taxes (or increasing subsidies) on state firms reduces income inequality (measured by the Gini coefficient) at least during the initial stages of transition. This kind of reduction also implies a slowdown of restructuring and lower unemployment in the initial stages.

Notes

Introduction

1. It is fair to say that Blanchard (1996) offers a similar broad view of transition. Blanchard, however, puts more emphasis on microeconomic incentives at the firm level, related to enterprise restructuring and privatization, while we focus more on stabilization and growth issues.

2. Frydman and Rapaczynski (1994) use this characterization for the process of privatization.

Chapter 1

1. Such useful classification is based both on objective indicators and on "educated judgment" obtained from economists working on the countries.

2. We will use the World Bank indicators because they are available on a yearly basis since 1989, thus allowing a dynamic analysis of the relation between reforms and economic performance.

3. Sahay and Végh (1996) and Fischer, Sahay, and Végh (1996) argue that in economies in transition, exchange-rate-based stabilization programs were associated with better performance in terms of both inflation and output.

4. Nevertheless, the evaluation of the wage policies is an important element to assess the forces at work during stabilization programs. Indeed, in most countries wages fell below the ceilings imposed by centralized wage policies, suggesting that wage moderation was affected by other constraints. Specifically, credit constraints exerted a crucial effect on wage determination. Evidence on Poland confirms this point (Calvo and Coricelli 1992; Pinto and van Wijnbergen 1995).

5. See also Tornell and Velasco (1995) for a critical view on the disciplining effects of fixed exchange rates.

6. Holdings of foreign currency in the form of cash are likely to be larger than official deposits in several countries. However, no data are available for these holdings.

7. Moreover, the initial boost to consumption and output of ERBs comes usually from credibility issues, namely the expectation of reversal of the stabilization program and the collapse of the exchange rate. Thus, another possibility is that programs were more credible in transition economies than in Latin America.

8. Frydman and Wellisz (1991), using a simple cost-push model based on an input-output table, were able to predict well the increase in January 1990 of producer prices in Poland.

9. Under fixed exchange rates, base money becomes endogenous. The lack of bond markets limits the possibility of sterilizing changes in base money due to changes in international reserve. In PCPEs, however, the central bank was in a very strong domestic asset position in the form of refinancing credit to commercial banks. Moreover, the central bank could affect broad money by affecting the money multiplier.

10. See Calvo (1992) on the drawbacks of using the interest rate as a tool to reduce inflation.

11. These estimates were generated by computing input costs and output prices at world prices. Of course, these estimates have to be regarded with caution, as they assume given productivities.

12. Of course, the indirect effects of those activities on production of input suppliers must also be taken into account.

13. For instance, if Russia began its program in 1992 while Poland began its in 1990, the dates for Poland will be shifted two years ahead.

14. This point is forcefully made by Sachs (1994) in the discussion of the comparison between China and Eastern Europe. However, it is striking that the issue is generally neglected in the analysis of Central and Eastern European reforms by Sachs himself. The implicit assumption of homogeneity of the sample of Central and Eastern European countries is untenable.

15. The generic statement that the success of Poland in the last few years is the outcome of the "shock therapy" followed in 1990 is a case in point (Friedman and Johnson 1995; Balcerowicz 1995).

Chapter 2

1. This covariation of bank and interenterprise credit can be interpreted as an indication of a nonfinancial shock to the economy, which, by affecting output, negatively determined a decline in the demand for every form of credit. However, the interpretation endorsed in this chapter attributes the covariation to the sudden increase in credit risk in the economy, resulting from the introduction of hard budget constraints (Calvo and Coricelli 1993). Interestingly, even for market economies, Oliner and Rudebusch (1993) have argued the importance of a broad credit view, in contrast to a bank-lending view. Accordingly, what would

matter for economic activity is the contraction of all forms of credit and not the contraction of some part of it that could be compensated by other forms of credit.

2. Some caution should be used in interpreting the data. Indeed, especially for inputs, data for the first quarter of 1990 likely understate the ratio of inventories to sales. Given that the rotation of inventories was larger than a month's worth of sales at end-1989—in fact, close to two months' worth—the price jump of January 1990 increased the value of sales, while part of the inventory stock was still valued at the old prices. Even taking an average price, however, would still give a sharp drop of input inventories at the beginning of 1990. However, a more reasonable figure is the one for end-1990, which indicates a ratio of input inventories to sales almost 50 percent lower than at end-1989. Note that measuring problems are much less serious for finished-good inventories, the rotation of which is less than two weeks.

3. This is an important reason why the interpretation of the view exposed in Calvo and Coricelli as supply-side is partly misleading. A more faithful interpretation puts enterprises rather than households at center stage, without implying that demand factors were irrelevant.

4. In the case of Romania there were continuous complaints by the authorities against firms that supposedly had large holdings of money and nevertheless were defaulting on their payments.

5. In 1992, for instance, out of 16,280 firms in the sample, 15,439 did not have short-term credit from banks. Out of 2,439 fully state-owned firms, 670 had short-term credit from banks.

6. In 1991, for instance, the credit-to-sales ratio was 13.74 percent for large firms, while it was 20.85 percent for small firms.

7. The coefficient on losses and profits should be considered together to obtain the role of net profits.

8. See Pinto et al. (1994) for a different view obtained from a small sample of surveyed firms.

9. Some of the results are also in line with those of Cornelli et al. (1996). However, there are important differences that in particular relate to the different behavior of leverage and the bank credit.

10. Interestingly, regressions on trade credit indicate that profitability enters with a negative sign also in the equation on trade debt. Thus, profitable firms tend to have low indebtedness, both with banks and with other firms.

11. From data on banks in Poland it turns out that, looking at stocks, new banks account for a large proportion of lending to private firms (more than 50 percent). However, taking into account the starting position of the old—mainly state-owned—banks, characterized by a portfolio almost entirely concentrated on state firms, flows also must be taken into account. Between 1990 and 1995 the flow of credit allocated to pri-

vate firms was of a magnitude similar to the flow to state firms. This implies a significant redistribution of credit in favor of private firms, given that state firms accounted for almost 100 percent of the initial credit portfolio. Thus, even the old banks contributed toward accommodating the growth of the private sector.

12. See Arnott and Stiglitz (1988) for an application to insurance markets. The view that trust plays a crucial role in market economies is becoming increasingly popular, at least among economic historians or sociologists (see Putnam 1993). Use of such a concept may be appealing for the analysis of radical system changes, such as in transition economies.

13. Of course, even in Hungary and Poland the system may be still rudimentary. Nevertheless, there is a secondary market, a few banks are involved in factoring operations, bills of exchange are used, and, finally, information on the credit-worthiness of firms is published in specialized magazines.

14. It is worth noting that in the CSFR at the outset of reforms, the ratio of net to gross arrears was much higher, in fact close to one in 1990. Only over time did the ratio decline, suggesting that a chain of arrears grew over time. In fact, while gross arrears registered a fivefold increase from 1990 to March 1992, net arrears increased by only 70 percent, a figure not far from the increase in prices. Therefore, the sharp real increase in gross arrears took place with practically no increase in real net debt positions of firms.

15. A first attempt at a regression analysis of micro data for Romania and Poland is contained in Calvo and Coricelli (1993, 1994). We extend that analysis on Poland by considering the evolution over time of the phenomenon. Moreover, we compare the features and determinants of interenterprise arrears with arrears in payments to other creditors, such as the state and the banks.

Chapter 3

1. Frydman and Rapaczynski (1994) use this characterization for the process of privatization.

2. We use a broad concept of capital, including both physical and human capital.

3. The definition discussed in chapter 1 is used here.

4. A sufficient condition for the UK curve to be hump-shaped, as in figure 1, is (see Chadha et al. 1993):

$$\frac{\partial E}{\partial U} \cdot \frac{U}{E} < \frac{1-\alpha}{\alpha}$$

5. Tanzi (1993), Kornai (1993), Chadha and Coricelli (1994), Aghion and Blanchard (1993).

6. Similar results obtain in the case of endogenous restructuring (see Aghion and Blanchard 1993, pp. 14-16). An interesting difference, however, is that in this case the transition may fail because of a too slow restructuring implied by the deficit financing.

7. Of course, the example with exogenous closure of the state sector neglects the important connection between fiscal constraints and the endogenous response of the state sector. In the version of the Aghion-Blanchard model with endogenous restructuring—wherein restructuring becomes a choice of state-firm insiders—loosening of the budget constraint increases the likelihood of successful restructuring, but this is achieved through slower restructuring. Indeed, a loosening of the budget constraint will determine a reduction of taxes on both state and private firms. State firms can keep a higher number of workers, slowing down the reallocation of labor from state to private sectors. Thus, in the Aghion-Blanchard model, with endogenous restructuring, fiscal pressure can be used to foster the restructuring of the economy, although an excessive tightening of the government budget may jeopardize the restructuring process.

8. For private sector growth we use the quantitative indicators from the World Bank. See chapter 1 for a discussion of such indicators. We split the sample as follows: low private sector development, indicator from 0 to 0.5; high development, indicator from 0.6 to 1.

9. This section is a revised version of Coricelli (1996).

10. The Czech Republic, Hungary, Poland, and Slovakia belong to the fast reformer group, while Bulgaria and Romania belong to the slow reformer group. The classification is admittedly crude and should be taken as merely indicative. The classification is based on indicators in three areas: (1.) enterprise restructuring and privatization; (2.) market reform: price liberalization, internal and external competition; (3.) financial sector reform (see EBRD 1994, p. 11).

11. The average government expenditures at the end of the 1980s for the following countries was 49 percent of GDP: Austria, Denmark, Finland, France, Germany, Portugal, Ireland, the Netherlands, Norway, Spain, Sweden, and the United Kingdom.

12. In Poland, for instance, the number of new pensions increased sharply in 1990 and 1991, from 437,000 in 1989 to 653,000 in 1990 and 912,000 in 1991, while the number of people reaching retirement age was roughly constant (133,000 in 1989, 144,000 in 1990, and 138,000 in 1991) (Coricelli, Hagemejer, and Rybinski 1995).

13. Sachs (1995) attributes to such power one of the main reasons for the electoral successes in the region of parties emanating from old communist parties and running on programs favoring the maintenance of social expenditures.

14. Discretionary policy changes are derived by subtracting from the total change in tax revenue to GDP the endogenous effect calculated by applying unchanged tax rates to the change in the tax base (IMF 1994).

15. Data are from a 3-digit level dataset from the Polish statistical office. As branches with fewer than three firms are excluded, the sample does not capture the whole economy.

References

Aghion, P., and O. Blanchard. 1993. On the speed of transition in Central Europe. Working Paper 6. London: European Bank for Reconstruction and Development.

Aldes, A. F., M. Kiguel, and N. Liviatan. 1995. Disinflation without output decline: Tales of exchange-rate-based stabilizations. In R. Holzmann, J. Gacs, and G. Winkler (eds.), *Output decline in Eastern Europe: Unavoidable, external influence, or homemade?* Dordrecht: Kluwer.

Anderson, R., E. Berglof, and K. Mizei. 1996. Banking sector development in Central and Eastern Europe. *EPI Forum* n.1. Centre for Economic Policy Research and Institute for East-West Studies.

Arnott, R., and J. Stiglitz. 1988. Dysfunctional nonmarket institutions and the market. National Bureau of Economic Research Working Paper n. 2666. Chicago.

Atkinson, A. B. and J. Micklewright. 1992. *Economic transformation in Eastern Europe and the distribution of income.* Cambridge: Cambridge University Press.

Barbone, L., and D. Marchetti. 1994. Economic transformation and the fiscal crisis. Policy Research Working Paper n. 1286. Washington, D.C.: World Bank.

Begg, D., and R. Portes. 1993. Enterprise debt and economic transformation: Financial restructuring of the state sector in Central and Eastern Europe. In C. Mayer and X. Vives (eds.), *Financial intermediation in Europe.* Cambridge: Cambridge University Press.

Belka, M., S. Estrin, M. Schaffer, and I. J. Singh. 1994. Enterprise adjustment in Poland: Evidence from a survey of 200 private, privatized and state-owned firms. Policy Research Department. Washington, D.C.: World Bank.

Berg, A., and O. Blanchard. 1994. Stabilization and transition: Poland, 1990–91. In O. Blanchard, K. Froot, and J. Sachs (eds.), *The transition in Eastern Europe.* Chicago: National Bureau of Economic Research (NBER).

Blanchard, O. 1996. *The economics of transition.* Oxford: Oxford University Press.

Blanchard, O., and S. Fischer. 1989. *Lectures on macroeconomics.* Cambridge, Mass.: MIT Press.

Blejer, M. I., G. Calvo, F. Coricelli, and A. Gelb (eds.). 1993. *Eastern Europe in transition: From recession to growth?* World Bank Discussion Papers, n. 196. Washington, D.C.: World Bank.

Blejer, M. I., and F. Coricelli. 1995. *The making of economic reform in Eastern Europe: Conversations with leading reformers in Poland, Hungary and the Czech Republic.* Aldershot: Edward Elgar.

Bonin, J., and M. Schaffer. 1995. Banks, firms, bad debts and bankruptcy in Hungary 1991-94. Discussion Paper n. 234. London: Centre for Economic Performance.

Bruno, M. 1993. Stabilization and reform in Eastern Europe: Preliminary evaluation. In M. I. Blejer, G. Calvo, F. Coricelli, and A. Gelb (eds.), *Eastern Europe in transition: From recession to growth?* World Bank Discussion Papers, n. 196. Washington, D.C.: World Bank.

Burda, M. 1993. Unemployment, labor market institutions, and structural change in Eastern Europe. *Economic Policy,* no. 16: 101-38

Calvo, G. A. 1978. Urban unemployment and wage determination in LDCs: Trade unions in the Harris-Todaro model. *International Economic Review* 19, n. 1: 65-81.

———.1992. Are interest rates effective for stopping high inflation? Some skeptical notes. *World Bank Economic Review,* n.1: 55-69.

Calvo, G. A., and F. Coricelli. 1992. Stabilizing a previously centrally planned economy: Poland 1990. *Economic Policy,* n. 14: 176-226

———.1993. Output collapse in Eastern Europe: The role of credit. International Monetary Fund *Staff Papers* 40 (March): 35-52.

———. 1994. Credit market imperfections and output response in previously centrally planned economies. In G. Caprio, D. Folkerts-Landau, and T. Lane (eds.), *Building sound finance in emerging market economies.* Washington, D.C.: International Monetary Fund and World Bank.

Calvo G. A., and M. Kumar. 1994. Money demand, bank credit, and the economic performance in former socialist economies. International Monetary Fund, *Staff Papers* 41 (June): 314-339.

Calvo G. A., R. Sahay, and C. Végh. 1995. Capital flow in Central and Eastern Europe: Evidence and policy options. Working Paper Series, no. 57. Washington D.C.: International Monetary Fund.

Caprio, G., D. Folkerts-Landau, and T. Lane (eds.). 1994. *Building sound finance in emerging market economies.* Washington, D.C.: International Monetary Fund and World Bank.

Carlin, W., J. Van Reenen, and T. Wolfe. 1994. Enterprise restructuring in the transition: An analytical survey of case study evidence from Central and Eastern Europe. Working Paper n. 14. London: European Bank for Reconstruction and Development.

Chadha, B., and F. Coricelli. 1994. Fiscal constraints and the speed of transition. Discussion Paper Series, n. 993. London: Centre for Economic Policy Research.

———. 1995. Unemployment, investment and sectoral reallocation. Discussion Paper Series, n. 1110. London: Centre for Economic Policy Research.

Clifton, E., and M. Kahn. 1993. Interenterprise arrears in transforming economies: The case of Romania. International Monetary Fund, *Staff Papers,* 40 (September) 680-96.

Cohen, D. 1995. The transition in Russia: Success (privatization, low unemployment) and failures (mafia, liquidity constraints): A theoretical analysis. Paris: CEPREMAP Working Papers, n.7.

Commander, S., and F. Coricelli (eds.). 1995. *Unemployment, restructuring and the labor market in Eastern Europe and Russia.* Washington, D.C.: EDI Development Studies.

Commander, S., F. Coricelli, and K. Staher. 1992. Wage and employment setting in economies in transition. In G. Winkler (ed.), *Central and Eastern Europe: Roads to growth.* Washington, D.C.: International Monetary Fund.

Commander, S., and R. Jackman. 1994. Providing social benefits in Russia: Redefining the roles of firms and government. Vienna: CEPR/IAS conference, Social protection and the enterprise in transitional economies.

Corbo, V., F. Coricelli, and J. Bossak (eds.). 1991. *Reforming Central and Eastern European economies: Initial results and challenges.* Washington, D.C.: World Bank.

Coricelli, F. 1996. Fiscal constraints, reform strategies, and the speed of transition: The case of Central and Eastern Europe. Discussion Paper, n. 1339. London: Centre for Economic Policy Research.

Coricelli, F., L. De la Calle, and B. Pinto. 1990. Poland: Macroeconomic policy in the second phase of the reform program. Washington, D.C.: World Bank.

Coricelli, F., K. Hagemejer, and K. Rybinski. 1995. Poland. In S. Commander, and F. Coricelli (eds.), *Unemployment, restructuring and the labor market in Eastern Europe and Russia*. Washington, D.C.: EDI Development Studies.

Coricelli, F., and R. Rocha. 1991. Stabilization programs in Eastern Europe: A comparative analysis of the Polish and Yugoslav programs of 1990. In V. Corbo, F. Coricelli, and J. Bossak (eds.), *Reforming Central and Eastern European economies: Initial results and challenges*. Washington, D.C.: The World Bank.

Cornelli, F., R. Portes, and M. Schaffer. 1996. The capital structure of firms in Central and Eastern Europe. Discussion Paper Series, n. 1392. London: Centre for Economic Policy Research.

De Gregorio, J., and F. Sturzenegger. 1994. Financial markets and inflation under imperfect information. Washington, D.C.: International Monetary Fund Working Paper, 94/63.

De Melo, M., C. Denizer, and A. Gelb. 1995. From plan to market: Patterns of transition. Washington, D.C.: World Bank.

———. 1996. Transition to date: A comparative overview. Washington, D.C.: World Bank.

Dewatripont, M., and G. Roland. 1996. Transition as a process of large-scale institutional change. *Economics of Transition* 4, n. 1: 1–30.

———. 1992a. Economics reform and political constraints. *Review of Economic Studies* 59: 703–730.

———. 1992b. The virtues of gradualism and legitimacy in the transition to a market economy. *Economic Journal* 102: 1207–23.

Earle, J. 1994. Employee benefits and labor market behavior. Working Paper n. 2. Prague: Central European University, Economics Department.

Earle, J., R. Frydman, A. Rapaczynski, and J. Turkewitz .1994. *Small privatization: The transformation of retail trade and consumer services in the Czech Republic, Hungary and Poland*. Budapest: Central European University Press.

Estrin, S., M. Schaffer, and I.J. Singh. 1994. The provision of social benefits in state-owned, privatized and private firms in Poland. Working Paper n. 606. London: Centre for Economic Performance.

European Bank for Reconstruction and Development (EBRD). 1995. *Transition Report 1995: Investment and enterprise development*. London.

Fajith, L., and J. Lakatos. 1994. Fringe benefits in transition in Hungary. Vienna: CEPR/IAS conference, Social protection and the enterprise in transitional economies.

Farmer, R. 1993. *The macroeconomics of self-fulfilling prophecies.* Cambridge, Mass.: MIT Press.

Fischer, S., R. Sahay, and C. Végh. 1996. From transition to market: Evidence and growth prospects.Washington, D.C.: International Monetary Fund.

Friedman, E.J., and S. Johnson. 1995. Complementarities and optimal reform. Durham, NC: Duke University.

Frydman, R., and S. Wellisz. 1991. The ownership-control structure and the behavior of Polish enterprises during the 1990 reforms: Macroeconomic measures and microeconomic responses. In V. Corbo, F. Coricelli, and J. Bossak (eds.), *Reforming Central and Eastern European economies: Initial results and challenges.* Washington, D.C.:The World Bank.

Frydman, R., and A. Rapaczynski. 1994. *Privatization in Eastern Europe: Is the state withering away?* Budapest: Central European University Press.

Garvy, G. 1966. *Money, banking and credit in Eastern Europe.* Federal Reserve of New York.

Gavin, M. 1993. Unemployment and the economics of gradualist policy reform. New York: Columbia University.

Grosfeld, I. 1994. Financial systems in transition: Is there a case for a bank based system? Discussion Paper n. 1062. London: Centre for Economic Policy Research.

Halpern, L., and C.Wyplosz. 1995. Equilibrium real exchange rates in transition.Discussion Paper n. 1145. London: Centre for Economic Policy Research.

Hare, P. 1994. Social protection and its implications for enterprise restructuring. Vienna: CEPR/IAS conference, Social protection and the enterprise in transitional economies.

Holzmann, R. 1994. Funded and private pensions for Eastern European countries in transition? Research paper n. 9404. University of Saarland, Europa Institut.

Holzmann, R., J. Gacs, and G. Winkler (eds.). 1995. *Output decline in Eastern Europe: Unavoidable, external influence or homemade?* Dordrecht: Kluwer.

Ickes, B., and R. Ryterman. 1992. The interenterprise arrears crisis in Russia. *Post Soviet Affairs* 8: 331-61.

International Monetary Fund (IMF). 1994a. Eastern Europe—Factors underlying the weakening performance of tax revenues. Washington, D.C.: Working Paper Series, WP 94/104.

———. 1994b. *World Economic Outlook.* Washington, D.C.

Kehoe, P. 1995. Comments. *NBER Macroeconomics Annual,* n.1.

Kiguel, M., and N. Liviatan. 1991. Stopping inflation: The experience of Latin America and Israel and the implications for Central and Eastern Europe. In V. Corbo, F. Coricelli, and J. Bossak (eds.), *Reforming Central and Eastern European economies: Initial results and challenges.* Washington, D.C.: World Bank.

King, R. G., and R. Levine. 1993. Finance, entrepreneurship, and growth: Theory and evidence. *Journal of Monetary Economics* 32: 513-42.

Kornai, J. 1992. The postsocialist transition and the State: Reflections in the light of Hungarian fiscal problems. *American Economic Review,* Papers and Proceedings (May): 2-21.

———. 1993. Transformational recession: A general phenomenon examined through the example of Hungary's developments. Discussion Paper n. 1, Collegium Budapest.

Mc Kinnon, R. 1991. *The order of economic liberalization: Financial control in the transition to a market economy.* Baltimore: John Hopkins University Press.

———. 1993. Gradual versus rapid liberalization in socialist economies: The problem in macroeconomic control. In M. Bruno, and B. Pleskovic (eds.), *Proceedings of the World Bank Annual Conference on Development Economics,* Washington, D.C.

Micklewright, J., and G. Nagy. 1995. Unemployment insurance and incentives in Hungary. Discussion Paper Series, n. 1118. London: Centre for Economic Policy Research.

Milanovic, B. 1996. *Income, inequality, and poverty during the transition.* Washington, D.C.: World Bank.

Murrell, P. 1992. Evolution in economics and in the economic reform of the centrally planned economies. In C. Clague, and G. Raisser (eds.), The emergence of market economies in Eastern Europe, 35-53. Cambridge: Blackwell.

———. 1995. The transition according to Cambridge, Mass. *Journal of Economic Literature* (March): 164-178.

Newbery, D.M. 1994. Optimal tax rates and tax design during systemic reform. IPR67. Washington, D.C.: Institute for Policy Reform.

Oliner, S., and G. Rudebusch. 1993. Is there a bank credit channel for monetary policy? Washington, D.C.: Federal Reserve Discussion Paper.

Pinto, B., M. Belka, and S. Krajewski. 1993. Transforming state enterprises in Poland: Evidence on adjustment by manufacturing firms. *Brookings Papers on Economic Activity*, n. 1: 213-70.

Pinto, B., and S. van Wijnbergen. 1995. Ownership and corporate control in Poland: Why state firms defied the odds? Discussion Paper Series, n. 1273. London: Centre for Economic Policy Research.

Przeworski, A. 1991. *Democracy and the market: Political and economic reforms in Eastern Europe and Latin America.* Cambridge: Cambridge University Press.

Putnam, R. 1993. *Making democracy work.* Princeton: Princeton University Press.

Rodrik, D. 1995. The dynamics of political support for reform in economies in transition. Discussion Paper Series, n. 1115. London: Centre for Economic Policy Research.

————. 1993. Making sense of the Soviet trade shock in Eastern Europe: A framework and some estimates. In M. I. Blejer, G. Calvo, F. Coricelli, and A. Gelb (eds.), *Eastern Europe in transition: From recession to growth?* Washington, D.C.: World Bank Discussion Papers, n. 196.

Rostowski, J. 1993. The interenterprise debt explosion in the former Soviet Union: Causes, consequences, cures. *Communist Economies and Economic Transformation* 5, n. 2: 131-59.

Sachs, J. 1995. Article in *Transition.* Washington, D.C.: World Bank.

————. 1996. The transition at mid-decade. *American Economic Review, Papers and Proceedings* (May): 128-33.

Sahay, R., and C. Végh. 1996. Inflation and stabilization in transition economies: An analytical interpretation of the evidence. *Journal of Policy Reform*, n. 1.

Sargent, T. 1982. The ends of four big inflations. In R. Hall (ed.), *Inflation: Causes and effects.* National Bureau of Economic Research. Chicago: University of Chicago Press.

Scarpetta, S., T. Boeri, and A. Reutersward. 1993. Unemployment benefit systems and active labor market policies in Central and Eastern Europe: An overview. Paris: OECD conference, The persistence of unemployment in Central and Eastern Europe.

Schaffer, M.E. 1995. Government subsidies to enterprises in Central and Eastern Europe: Budgetary subsidies and tax arrears. Discussion Paper Series, n. 1114. London: Centre for Economic Policy Research.

Tanzi, V. 1993. Fiscal policy and the economic restructuring of economies in transition. Working Paper Series, WP 93/22. Washington, D.C.: International Monetary Fund.

Tornell, A., and A. Velasco. 1995. Fixed versus flexible exchange rates: Which provides more fiscal discipline? New York: C. V. Starr Center for Applied Economics, New York University.

Townsend, R. 1990. *Financial structure and economic organization: Key elements and patterns in theory and history.* Oxford: Basil Blackwell.

van Wijnbergen, S. 1994. On the role of banks in enterprise restructuring: The Polish example. Discussion Paper Series, n. 898. London: Centre for Economic Policy Research.

Winkler, G. 1992. Central and Eastern Europe: Roads to Growth. Washington, D.C.: International Monetary Fund and Bank of Austria.

World Bank. 1994. *Hungary; Structural reforms for sustainable growth.* Washington, D.C.: Country Operations, Central Europe Department.

―――. 1994. *Poverty in Poland.* Washington, D.C.: Country Operations, Central Europe Department.

Index

Aldes, A. F., 19
arrears: 11, 38; causes of, 76; chain of, 84; gross, 80; and inflation, 56; net, 80; and soft budget constraints, 76; tax, 132; and transfer of liquidity, 78; and transition, 76, 84; velocity of circulation, 63

bank credit: constraints on, 57; equilibrium, 50-1; and interenterprise credit, 52, 56; mathematical expression of, 57; and price liberalization, 45-6; reallocation of, 38-40; restriction of, 37-8; and trade credit, 6-7
bankruptcy, 132
banks: and arrears, 75; and automatic financing, 6, 38; behavior of, 70; as engine of change, 74; recapitalization of, 60, 66
"big-bang" program, 11, 28, 143
Bulgaria, 123, 126, 127

Calvo, G., 55, 57-8, 74
Central and Eastern Europe: and fiscal balance, 117; historical transformation of, 1; macroeconomic performance in, 11
central planning: and trade credit, 6, 38; transition from, 5, 39-40, 143
circularity, 6
Cobb-Douglas production function, 89, 90
competition, 24

Cornelli, F., 70
Council for Mutual Economic Assistance (CMEA), 19
credit: allocation of, 66-7; contracts, 5; and demand for money, 57; tightening of, 4, 6, 68-74
credit markets, 5; development of, 64; importance of, 64
credit overhang, 43-4
Czech Republic: exchange rate policy of, 18; privatization in, 123; revenue structure of, 127; size of government in, 123; and velocity of circulation, 61

De Gregorio, J., 61
De Melo, M., 33
decapitalization, 95
decentralization, 43
demonetization, 6, 38
Denizer, C., 33
devaluation, 9, 24, 26
Dewatripont, M., 1-2
disintermediation, 39

economic transition: 3-4, 7, 35-6; and adjustment costs, 92; and decline of state employment, 100; and distribution of labor, 99; driving force of, 92; and fiscal pressures, 117; income distribution during, 140-1; and market creation, 2; model of, 89-99; as process of evolution, 2, 5, 7, 86; and reallocation of resources, 86, 101-2;

and restructuring, 106; theory of, 2–3; and unemployment, 86, 142

elasticity, 59, 64, 91

employment subsidies, 110

equilibrium, 43; and arrears, 76, 84; bank credit, 50–1; cash, 50; in labor market, 92–3, 98; and low output, 40; in money market, 25; money-only; 52–5, 70; trade credit, 50–1, 52; Walrasian model of, 2

European Bank for Reconstruction and Development (EBRD), 117, 121

exchange rates: fixed, 36, 17–8, 20, 24; flexible, 16–8, 24

financial markets: and central planning, 5; characteristics of, 66; crucial role of 37; and restructuring, 28; underdevelopment of, 5, 10, 37

firms: and arrears, 78; nonviable 27, 28; and provision of social benefits, 125, 138–9; subsidies to, 11, 60; types of, 40–2; viable, 39, 66

fiscal deficits, 17

fiscal externality, 103

fiscal policy, 3, 10–1, 94, 98

former Soviet Union (fSU): and choice of exchange rate regime, 18; and income distribution, 136, 138–9; macroeconomic performance of, 11; postreform experience of, 29; and stabilization of inflation, 20–1; and stabilization programs, 8; unemployment in, 139

Frydman, R., 2

Gelb, A., 33

Gini coefficient, 140, 142, 145

gradualism, 1

gross domestic product (GDP): aggregate, 140; and budget deficits, 120, 121; and changes in employment, 88; and fixed exchange rates, 17; and liberalization, 33; and social security contributions, 130; and wages, 42, 125

Halpern, L., 26

hard budget constraints, 11, 28, 29, 113

human capital, 92–3, 106, 140

Hungary: arrears in, 77; bank credit in, 67, 70; budget deficits in, 66; capital expenditures in, 126; exchange rate policy of, 18; pensions in, 129; revenue structure of, 127; size of government in, 123; social security contribution in, 130; stabilization programs of, 16; trade credit in, 5, 71–2, 77; velocity of circulation in, 61

implosion, trade, 21–2

incentives: for commercial banks, 60; improvement in, 28; microeconomic, 2, 78, 84; and restructuring, 109

income: distribution of 135–9, 142; inequality of, 136, 140, 142; policy, 10

inflation: and arrears, 56, 60; causes of, 60; and macroeconomic performance, 4; and money demand, 60–1; and output, 57–9; and stabilization programs, 9–10, 13–8, 23; threshold of, 61

interfirm exchanges, 6

International Monetary Fund (IMF), 1, 9

inventory, initial, 49–50

investment: models of, 92-4; private, 94, 98, 103; public, 113, 125; in restructuring capital stock, 28; and self-financing of working capital, 39
Israel, 10

Kiguel, M., 13, 19
Krugman, Paul, 1
Kumar, M., 57-8
Kuznets curve, 7, 135, 140, 142

labor reallocation, 140
labor market equilibrium, 92
Laffer curve, 60
liberalization: economic, 4-5; prereform, 117; of prices, 10, 12, 22-4, 26, 36, 45; of trade, 12, 22
liquidity: and bank credit, 58; constraints, 10, 41, 58, 65, 83, 88; of enterprises, 57; and input inventories, 48; monetary policy, 38; and output, 37; transfer of, 74, 78, 80
Liviatan, N., 13, 19
loanable funds, 57-60

market discipline, 6
Mexico, 10
monetary exchanges, 5
monetary overhang, 23-4, 43-5, 49, 64
monetary policy, 10-1, 56, 76-85
money demand, 57-60
Murrel, P., 2

output collapse, 19-21

pensions, 129-30
Poland: arrears in, 77; bank credit in, 67-9; and bank restructuring scheme, 75; budget deficits in, 66; capital expen-
diture in, 126; credit in 5, 6; demand for money in, 59; elasticity of output in, 64; and exchange rate policy, 18; inflation tax in, 60; interest rates in, 66; pensions in, 129; and price liberalization, 47-8; size of government in, 123; and social benefits, 125; and structure of revenues, 127; trade credit in, 71-2, 74, 77
policy credibility, 27-28
populism, 1
previously centrally planned economies (PCPEs): and credit policy, 27; decline in output of, 8; initial inventories of, 49; institutional characteristics of, 3; stabilization programs in, 77; trade credit markets in, 74
price jump, 25-27
privatization, 4; large-scale, 2; and output levels, 95; and unemployment, 95, 98
Przeworski, A., 142

Rapaczynski, A., 2
reform: and initial conditions, 29-34; institutional, 3; pace of, 8; strategies of, 13, 34-6; structural, 3
Rocha, Roberto, 26
Roland, G., 1-2
Romania: arrears in, 77; capital expenditure in, 124-5, 126; size of government in, 123; trade credit in, 78; velocity of circulation in, 62

Sachs, J., 4
Sahay, R., 43
Samuelson, Paul, 1
shibboleths, 1
shock therapy, 1

Slovak Republic: privatization in, 123; size of government in, 123; velocity of circulation in, 61

socialism, 136

social services, provision of, 113

soft budget constraints, 2, 11, 27, 29, 76

stabilization, 4; and collapse of output, 8; exchange-rate-based, 9, 10, 13–6, 18–9, 26; instruments of, 11–2; macroeconomic, 2, 9; money-based, 9, 13–5, 19

Sturzenegger, F., 61

subsidies: and demise of CMEA, 19; elimination of, 28; increase of, 144, 145; and inflation, 60; output, 112–3; reduction of, 11, 118, 120, 131, 135; and restructuring, 110; wage, 110

supply-side disruptions, 21–2

Tobin, James, 25

trade credit: and bank credit, 52; and central planning, 6–7; development of, 38–9; and equilibrium, 51–2; and trade sector, 46; voluntary, 6

trade implosion, 21–2

transition paths, 86–9

Ukraine: arrears in, 56; bank credit in, 63, 64; foreign currency deposits in, 18; trade credit in, 78, velocity of circulation in, 62–3

uncertainty, 23–4, 27–8

unemployment: benefits, 110, 112; and budget deficits, 120; and economic restructuring, 7–8, 87, 102–3, 106–8, 112; fiscal implications of, 121; optimal rate of, 87, 88–9; and output, 107, 115–6; and private sector, 91, 103, 115–6, 117; and restructuring, 106; social impact of, 135; and speed of privatization, 123; and structural change, 121; and tax rates, 98–9, 101

United Kingdom, 136

VAT, 127

Végh, C., 43

velocity of circulation, 61–2

wage policy, 10

Walrasian general equilibrium model, 2

World Bank, 1, 30, 34, 117

Wyplosz, C., 26

Yugoslavia, 10, 26

*Macroeconomic Policies and the Development
of Markets in Transition Economies*

was designed and composed by Judit Mihala
in Garamond 11 pt
printed and bound by

Gyomai Kner Nyomda Rt.
in its 115th year of operation
on 80-gram Kossuth paper, bound in Holland linen
and published by

Central European University Press